WENTWORTH CHESWILL'S RIDE

Chasing a Would-Be American Folk Hero

JOHN HERMAN

MOONLIGHT BRIDGE BOOKS

Newmarket, New Hampshire

First edition, April 2024

ISBN: 979-8-218-40045-3

Moonlight Bridge Books
Newmarket, New Hampshire

Wentworth Cheswill Appreciation Society

Cover illustration by Lisa Cordner

To Danielle, Emrys, and Morgan

ACKNOWLEDGMENTS

Thank you to the New Market Historical Society, the Lamprey Arts and Culture Alliance, Richard Alperin, John Carmichael, Kris Carmichael, Michael Provost, Jonathan Kiper, Tiara Lee, Brian Ward, Patrick Reynolds, Charlotte DiLorenzo, Larry Doyle, Jack Herman, Linda Herman, Justin Herman, Deborah Douville, Krista Brown Robertson, Tito Jackson, Julian Smith, Lisa Cordner, and all the family and friends who have supported my efforts to learn about Wentworth Cheswill so that I might spread the word.

PREFACE

> "One, if by land, and two, if by sea;
> And I on the opposite shore will be,
> Ready to ride and spread the alarm
> Through every Middlesex village and farm,
> For the country folk to be up and to arm."
> —Henry Wadsworth Longfellow, *Paul Revere's Ride*

Four years after his midnight ride, Paul Revere was charged with cowardice and insubordination, court-martialed, and dismissed from the militia. He and his men fled without orders from a botched military operation at the Penobscot Bay in Maine, since called the worst naval disaster in America outside of Pearl Harbor.

After the terrible affair, Revere returned to Boston where he was placed under house arrest until the whole debacle could be investigated. He claimed the charges were political. He was acquitted two years later, but his involvement in the most disastrous failure of the Revolutionary War could have forever soiled any memory of him—if not for a poem.

Written by Henry Wadsworth Longfellow eighty-five years after the events it described, the poem was published in *The Atlantic Monthly* in

1861. It made no mention of Paul Revere's war exploits. Instead the poem fictionalized a midnight ride he took as a messenger for the Committee of Safety as the revolution began. While literary critics preferred another poem in the collection, *The Saga of King Olaf*, which author Nathaniel Hawthorne described as "inscrutable magic," this poem, *Paul Revere's Ride*, dramatically increased in popularity in the decades that followed, plucking a man from relative obscurity and turning him into an American folk hero.

In 1883, over a hundred years after Paul Revere's eponymous ride, the hype had grown so much that a nationwide contest was held to identify a sculptor to honor the celebrated patriot. Utah-born Cyrus Dallin was selected, but the project endured a long bout of funding issues. The monument was finally revealed to the public in 1940, 57 years later. Today it stands in Boston's Paul Revere Mall.

Over the years, generations embraced Longfellow's poem. Paul Revere was cemented into the story of early America. He is still honored and remembered in countless ways. The house where he lived is one of the oldest surviving buildings in Boston. It offers exhibits related to his life and the events of his time. The city of Revere, located just north of Boston, is named after Paul Revere. Revere Beach, the first public beach in the nation, is also named in his honor. The USS Revere, a ship that served in World War II, had a bell that was cast from the same metal as the Liberty Bell and was named in honor of Paul Revere. It was the lead ship of the Paul Revere class of attack transports. The list goes on.

Without a poem or a warship to inspire curiosity, an interest in Wentworth Cheswill takes more effort. I first learned of him when I drove by New Hampshire Historical Highway Marker #209 on South Main Street in the town of Newmarket. The small green sign sits on the side of the road, overlooking the Cheswill family cemetery, a collection of thin, pale stones enclosed by a rock wall and a black iron gate displaying the name of Wentworth's daughter, Martha. From the marker, I learned that he was a teacher, a prolific community leader, a historian, and a pioneering archeologist. The marker also mentions he had a "negro" grandfather.

When I got home, I searched online for more information about him. There wasn't much. Several history blogs called Wentworth Cheswill the "Black Paul Revere." Being remembered for hundreds of years but only as a derivative of someone else struck me as deeply unfortunate. There was no historical home turned museum for me to visit. There was no statue. There was no beach. There wasn't even a poem. To be remembered at all is admirable, but surely the "Black Paul Revere" deserved to be recognized by his own name.

A poem worked for the original Paul Revere, so I endeavored to write one for Wentworth Cheswill.

First, I collected every publication I could find that referenced him. While there were no books solely dedicated to his life, there was a considerable amount of peripheral mentions. I will be name-dropping books and authors throughout these pages to encourage you to seek them out directly and support their work. I also went through academic papers that addressed Wentworth Cheswill and his extraordinary family. They were written by students at the nearby University of New Hampshire, where I too attended college. I will mention them too. I visited Wentworth Cheswill's handwritten journal of town records, which is kept at the Milne Special Collections and Archives at UNH's Dimond Library. I sought out old deeds and maps, and I transcribed centuries old legal papers from when Wentworth Cheswill was a county judge. Finally, I pieced it all together, every primary and secondary source I could get my hands on. It felt like I was chasing a would-be American folk hero who kept galloping off on horseback just as I greeted him.

Whenever I shared tales of Wentworth Cheswill with friends or family, they were astonished or skeptical. "Why haven't I heard of him already?" they asked. It was a fair question. He was relatively unknown—even in the town he helped shape. If he was so interesting, then where were all his admirers?

I hoped my poem could spur interest. Here is how it began:

> Read these words for I shall tell
> Of a man whose name should ring every bell,

For his story is revolutionary,
driven by a love for community and liberty.
Behold the life of Wentworth Cheswill!

It was of course an homage to *Paul Revere's Ride.*

Donning a tricorn hat, flanked by a talented upright bass player who owed me a favor, I performed my three page poem, *Wentworth Cheswill's Ride*, onstage at the Millspace, a community civic center I had a hand in developing in the revitalized Newmarket Mills less than a mile from the Cheswill family cemetery. As I had hoped, the poem garnered attention. Like me, many wanted to learn more about this 18th century mixed race archeologist, soldier, and judge, a man often cited as the first person of African descent elected to public office in the United States of America.

Early American history is full of recognizable names and faces. Their life stories are the origins of America itself. Since their passing, our founding fathers have had their faults minimized and their accomplishments elevated. Time heals all wounds. These men have been depicted in movies, embellished in paintings, poems, and statues. For the most part, their legacies remain unscathed. I am in no way suggesting that we replace their stories with new ones. I only suggest that there are others who can offer unique perspectives on the birth of the nation.

With his ability to enrich and broaden our understanding of early American history, I offer Wentworth Cheswill for consideration. Perhaps it's the teacher in me, but I believe we should always be on the lookout for stories that can enrich us with new perspectives about our collective past. Personally, I think he is worthy of attention. He was a teacher and a Revolutionary War veteran. He was a scholar and a historian. He helped establish the first library in his community. He was a prolific community leader. Like many of the leaders of his generation, he was a freemason. He performed some of the earliest archeological work in the country. There is so much to learn from him.

I only brought up Paul Revere's weakest moment to make a point. The truth is that Revere made contributions to the patriotic cause that were honorable and inspiring. He had a bad moment during the revolution, but who judges a man for running from certain death? He was a talented artisan of the period and he never trafficked or enslaved another human being. By 18th century American standards, he was very admirable, perhaps even worthy of the remembrance he has enjoyed for generations. My point was to deconstruct what elevated him to an American folk hero. Revere is celebrated in children's books. He has a museum and a statue, but it took more than a poem to get him there. It took dedication and devotion to an ideal. It took special care and persistence. History can be a hard sell when there are so many other things to concern ourselves in the modern world. Sometimes the wrong people are put on pedestals. In the case of Paul Revere, society seemed to get it right, but it took decades to get there and I still wonder about the many others who were left behind.

In school, my students treat any event that happened before they were born as if it was ancient history. Early America might as well be shelved with tales of pharaonic Egypt. I often remind myself of Harrison Ruffin Tyler, who is still alive at the time of my writing this sentence. He is the grandson of the 10th president of the United States of America, John Tyler, who was born in 1790. In just three generations of a single family, one can find themself back to the 18th century. Time is an illusion.

If thinking about the past in this way is a paradigm shift for you, then go ahead and have a cup of tea. Look longingly at the ocean and contemplate your own fleeting moment on Earth. I'll be here when you are ready. I think this book, my next step in spreading the word about Wentworth Cheswill, will be a lot more enjoyable if you regard the people within its pages as those who were just here among us. They only recently walked down the same streets under the same moonlight.

The book is short but dense. There are a lot of names and dates to digest. I also name the historians you should check out and I cite their work. I offer it all as a starting point for those who want to broaden their understanding of early American history through the lens of a fascinating individual and his family. The story of Wentworth Cheswill is one of mysterious family origins, admirable associations, and an astonishing life of service. He fought during the Battles of Saratoga, America's first major victory in the Revolutionary War. After his death, his reputation reached the U.S. Capitol, his public service cited in congressional debate over the Missouri Compromise. The high regard Wentworth Cheswill held for so many generations after his passing is a testimony to his character. This is the story of a man who made an impact in his community, a family that defied cultural obstacles, and a community that strove to make a difference.

I will start before Wentworth Cheswill was born, with the first person to take the name Cheswill. I will end this volume with a volcano that changed the world.

I hope you enjoy the ride.

~John Herman, April 2024

RICHARD CHESWILL

Beware, lest in the worm you crush
A brother's soul you find;
And tremble lest thy luckless hand
Dislodge a kindred mind.
                    —Anna L. Aikin, 1773

In 1717, Richard Cheswill of Exeter signed with a mark, for he could not read or write, confirming the purchase of twenty acres of land from Joseph Hilton. According to *Black Portsmouth: Three Centuries of African-American Heritage* by Mark J. Sammons and Valerie Cunningham, that purchase makes him the earliest known landowner of African descent in New Hampshire.

If there is a beginning to the Cheswill family saga, then this is it.

The land in question, granted in 1631 by King Charles I, had been claimed by the Hilton family since Edward Hilton, one of New Hampshire's first European settlers, explored the Piscataqua River in 1623. Eight years before the land transaction was made, Richard was released from enslavement by the David Lawrence family of Exeter. His origins prior to this pivotal moment are unknown, but it is likely Richard came to New England by way of Barbados. In 1708, correspondence from the colonial governor Joseph Dudley reported that there were seventy enslaved in the region. One year later, Daniel Defoe would break down the tiers of English society by "the great, who live profusely; the rich, who live plentifully; the middle sort, who live well; the working trades, who labour hard, but feel no want; the country people, farmers, etc. who fare indifferently; the poor that fare hard; the miserable, that really pinch and suffer want." If the English colonies followed that breakdown, then Richard was freed only to live in that last tier, that of the miserable.

To provide further historical context: The year Richard was freed was the same year Captain Woodes Rogers rescued privateer Alexander Selkirk from four years surviving alone on a remote island. Selkirk's harrowing experience would inspire Daniel Defoe's novel *Robinson Crusoe*, published 10 years later. It was the same year Bartolomeo di Francesco Cristofori of Italy introduced the "gravicembalo col piano e forte," a harpsichord able to play soft and loud, now called the piano. It was the same year the first hot-air balloon took flight. Invented by Brazilian priest Bartolomeu de Gusmãot, the balloon's notable third attempt nearly set fire to the palace of King John V of Portugal.

After being freed, Richard took the surname Cheswill. Or Cheswell. Or Caswell maybe. What he intended is not clear, but the name lived on, marking three remarkable generations. After the third generation, the spelling of the name changed from Cheswill to Cheswell, where it continued on for many generations more.

Exeter, where Richard lived, spanned the current towns of Exeter, Newmarket, Newfields, Epping, Brentwood, and Fremont. Back then much of the land would have been heavily wooded with European settlers living along the river banks and the forests inhabited by the indigenous Squamscott, an Algonquian people part of the southern Penacooks. Skirmishes between the settlers and indigenous families were common. Six years earlier, in 1703, Esther Wheelwright, the great-great granddaughter of Exeter's first settler John Wheelwright, was captured and brought to Canada against her will. Retaliatory actions were common and relationships would only worsen as treaties and land agreements between the colonists and various tribal speakers were often signed and broken.

In 1709, the Gilman family of Exeter built a garrison on the Squamscott River bank. The home, which still stands, features architectural details suggesting it had a portcullis, which is a vertical gate like the ones found in medieval fortifications. Like a castle entrance, the gate could be lowered whenever there was danger

Fear was an undercurrent the year Richard was freed.

Those who lived far from the Exeter meeting house were increasingly resistant to trekking miles through the woods for fellowship and governance. The journey was just too dangerous. There were no street lamps to guide the way as they crossed land inhabited by indigenous communities resisting displacement.

Despite all this, there was still a bit of beauty amidst the darkness.

According to the *Gazetteer of the State of New Hampshire* published by Eliphalet Merrill in 1817, the only light at dawn or dusk was the Aurora-borealis. Merrill wrote:

> This luminous appearance has been observed in all seasons of the year; in extreme heat and cold and all intermediate degrees. The colour of the streams is sometimes variegated with white, blue, yellow, and red, the lustre of which reflected from the snow, is an appearance highly beautiful and interesting.

During this time, the colonists were digging into the region both figuratively and literally. They were clearing land for fields while also establishing mills, utilizing knowledge of lumbering passed from Scottish indentured servants who were prisoners of war from 1650's Battle of Dunbar. According to Carol Walker Aten of the Exeter Historical Society in *A Brief History of African-Americans in Exeter*, "As some of these settlers established their own wealth, they accumulated enslaved people..." Colonial wealth led to enslavement. As historian Jody Fernald said in *Slavery in New Hampshire: Profitable godliness to racial consciousness*, "As some of the enslaved bought their freedom, some were willed their freedom by their enslavers, or earned their freedom through military service, the population of color in New Hampshire tried to navigate the still hierarchical world of free men with the disadvantage of their backgrounds in slavery."

This is the world in which Richard Cheswill of Exeter emerged.

Richard's life prior to his freedom is a mystery. He may have been an indentured servant or a victim of human trafficking from West Africa. His freedom would set an otherwise unlikely path for his bi-racial son Hopestill, who was free at birth. Hopestill would amass a considerable wealth of land and influence, building homes and taverns for merchants and sea captains in nearby Portsmouth. Like Richard, he would buy and sell land. Hopestill used his wealth to provide for his son, Wentworth, described as "yellow." Undoubtedly the most prosperous man in town when he died, Wentworth would be regarded as a wise leader. In just two generations, the Cheswill family transitioned from enslavement to community-wide reverence. It was an astonishing progression.

The Cheswill family name ended with Wentworth Cheswill—at least that specific spelling of the name. While Wentworth always spelled his own name *Cheswill*, as seen in signatures just two weeks before his death, his neighbor called him *Cheswell* on his last day. Wentworth's children went by Cheswell, not as he, his father, and his grandfather before him spelled it. In all of American history, only three would use the surname Cheswill, spelled in that particular way.

So, where did the name come from?

Historian Glen Knoblock wondered if Richard might have taken the name of someone who helped him after he was freed. Perhaps, as Knoblock speculated, it was the Caswells of the Isles of Shoals. Knoblock wrote in *African American Historic Burial Grounds and Gravesites of New England*, that, "In 1711 the first Caswells joined a hard-drinking, hard-working Shoals fishing community that was already a century old. But unlike many seasonal fishermen who commuted from Europe, the Caswells stayed. They survived the dangerous fishing trade and the brutal winters on the windswept rocks." It is possible that, after being freed, Richard sought work in nearby Portsmouth harbor, which led him to cross paths with the Caswells. The islands and its roster of former inhabitants still draw intrigue from historians and tourists alike.

Rumored to be Blackbeard the Pirate's honeymoon spot, the Isle of Shoals were later the setting for some grisly 1873 murders. Could these rough and tumble Caswells have inspired Richard's surname? Caswell is not Cheswill, but spelling was fluid in these times and Richard was illiterate. Frankly, we know little more about Richard other than that he had his son, Hopestill, in *about 1712.*

This would be the end of Richard Cheswill's portion of the book if it wasn't for a scandalous rumor that has trailed him for generations.

The rumor is muddled and can be downright confusing to sort out. It is the first instance of the sort of mythology that can trail the origins of a folk hero. While Richard could have remained an interesting footnote in New Hampshire history, things instead become mysterious. As the story goes, Richard, while enslaved, had a relationship with the daughter of the royal colonial governor and was cast into the wilderness to raise a child born of the affair.

The Cheswill family origin story is remarkable without this secret path to privilege, but the rumor persisted, even into the modern era. In 2005, U.S. Representative Jeb Bradley paid tribute to Wentworth Cheswill, referencing the alleged affair, saying that Wentworth's grandfather Richard had married a governor's daughter. "This union was considered a disgrace to the (governor's) family, who sent them away to the woods of New Hampshire," said Bradley.

As you will see, the story is almost certainly not true. The governor's daughter story may have originally started as a way to explain the extraordinary rise of the Cheswill family, but no research has led me to believe anything other than this: There was never a scandalous affair between the enslaved Richard of Exeter and a governor's daughter.

I mean, let's do the math.

The governor in power when Richard's son Hopestill was born (*about* 1712) was Joseph Dudley, half brother of the puritan poet Anne Bradstreet and son of the second governor of the Massachusetts Bay Colony. Newmarket historian Nellie Palmer George, who frequently wrote about Wentworth Cheswill, was a descendant of Governor Dudley, but, in all her writing about the Cheswill family, whose mansion house was rented to her parents when she was a child, she never once claimed to be related to the Cheswills themselves.

Often characterized by his involvement in the French and Indian Wars and prolonged arguments over the salaries of his officials, Joseph Dudley was a fairly unpopular governor. Some historians point to his disreputable governance as having planted the seeds that lead to the American Revolution itself. While the ultimate downfall of royal British rule in the colonies may have started with Dudley, he seems to have been fairly uncontroversial in New Hampshire.

During Dudley's administration, New Hampshire was part of the Province of Massachusetts Bay, but it was also its own thing, a unique governing region. This dual arrangement lasted from 1699 to 1741, and Dudley's rule of New Hampshire was generally uncontroversial, unlike the vitriol experienced to the south. He visited periodically, but in order for the rumor to have any kind of merit, one of his daughters would have to be in New Hampshire as well, if not Exeter, in *about 1712*, or nine months prior.

So, let's speculate.

Joseph Dudley had six daughters. If one had an affair with Richard, then I would bet on his daughter Katherine. She was 22 years old in 1712. Approximately two years after the birth of Richard's son, in April of 1714, Katherine married William Dummer, son of the first American born silversmith. After he died, Dummer, who was governor himself for a while, donated his estate to establish a school. That school played a big part in the Cheswill family story. Wentworth Cheswill was a member of its inaugural class. This was a rare privilege that set him on a remarkable life path. Only twenty-eight students from around New England were in that first class so his inclusion is astonishing. How did he get the opportunity to attend? Did perhaps Wentworth Cheswill's secret grandmother, Katherine Dudley Dummer, get him enrolled?

The short answer is no.

Joseph Dudley is not even the governor linked to the scandalous rumor. That honor goes to another. Ironically this other governor was linked to one of Joseph Dudley's New Hampshire visits. In 1713,

Dudley was in the region to sign the Treaty of Portsmouth, an agreement between the British royal government and the coastal indigenous populations of Maine and New Hampshire. Among the other signers of the treaty was a man named John Wentworth, a sea captain. He would go on to become lieutenant governor in 1717. This is the very year Richard Cheswill became the first land owner of African descent in the region. It is the Wentworth family that is referenced in the governor's daughter rumor. What better way to carry on the family secret than by naming the next child in the family Wentworth (Cheswill)?

All sensationalism aside, the Wentworth family had a strong presence in the lives of all the people of New Hampshire. John Wentworth served as the colonial lieutenant governor from 1717 to 1730, but it is most likely that Wentworth Cheswill was named after John Wentworth's son Benning Wentworth, New Hampshire's first royal governor independent of Massachusetts.

Benning took office in 1741. Wentworth Cheswill was born five years later. According to historian David E. Van Deventer in an entry on Benning Wentworth for the *Oxford Dictionary of National Biography*, Benning was "able to [both] maintain a family dynasty and Portsmouth's control of the prosperous mast trade for a generation" and he was "perhaps even British America's first political machine." Quite a few locals named their children after him. It was believed that naming a child after a powerful person might pass on some of their clout. My own great-great grandfather had the first and middle name George Washington. That doesn't mean I have a family connection to the first American president. Believe me. I checked.

While the timing doesn't work for his daughter to be involved in a scandalous affair with Richard, Benning Wentworth was no stranger to scandal himself. He married his 21 year old housekeeper after his wife of 25 years died. Henry Wadsworth Longfellow turned the May-to-December relationship into the poem *Lady Wentworth*, which ironically appeared in 1863 alongside his poem about Paul Revere. The critics still preferred *The Saga of King Olaf*, which president Theodore Roosevelt would later compare to *The Battle Hymn of the Republic*.

The third Governor Wentworth, Benning's nephew, was also named John. He was a contemporary of Wentworth Cheswill and too young for any daughter to be involved in the birth of Wentworth Cheswill's father, Hopestill. This second John Wentworth would be the last royal governor of New Hampshire. He escaped to Canada after patriots pointed a cannon at his front door.

The Wentworth family of governors may have been an inspiration to the Cheswills and nothing more. No scandalous affair needs to exist to explain the extraordinary path that the Cheswill family followed. It is more likely that Richard, Hopestill, and Wentworth were all ambitious in their own right. If anything, then their ambition was driven by a desire to stay out of reach of the cruel shadow of enslavement.

So, there you have it. Four governors, three governors named Wentworth, and none of them were likely to have inspired the rumor. It just is not likely the daughter of any governor (Wentworth or not) had a relationship with Richard. That the rumor exists is an interesting mystery in itself, hence my dedicating a few paragraphs to it. How far back the rumor goes is unknown, but it is referenced in the notes of historian Sylvia Fitts Getchell in a copy of the collected *History of Newmarket* by the Newmarket Club of Boston. It is possible the rumor started with them.

The Newmarket Club of Boston was a social club made up of Newmarket expatriates living in the greater Boston area in the early 20th century. These men and women so loved their historically rich stomping ground that they congregated, produced reports and events, and even wrote a town history, which they serially published in their hometown periodical, the *Newmarket Advertiser*.

According to *An Uncharted Town: Newmarket on the Lamprey—Historical Notes and Personal Sketches* by Joseph Harvey, the club was "organized in the spring of 1904 at the home of Charles H. Haley in Dorchester, Mass., in response to requests sent out by Mr. John E. Savage of Mattapan, Mass., and others." By the first winter meeting on March 2, 1905, events were regularly being attended "by nearly one hundred members." The club, practically a cult of Newmarket (mostly kidding), took an interesting turn after a year of meetings. As Joseph Harvey said, "It is a matter of surprise and regret that no adequate record has ever been compiled of this town, which early in the history of our state and nation played no small part." So that's exactly what the Newmarket Club of Boston set out to do. They composed a history.

While the club covered a lot of material in their *History of Newmarket* newspaper column, the mysterious identity of Richard's partner, mother of Hopestill, grandmother to the famed Wentworth Cheswill, was never directly addressed. Richard Cheswill's partner was a mystery to even them. Luckily others have made progress.

Currently, there is an agreed upon name for the woman who had a relationship with Richard Cheswill, and she wasn't a governor's daughter at all. Her name was Jane.

Before I introduce Jane, let me be clear that primary sources on the matter are nonexistent. Richard and Hopestill had the same surname (used by no one else), they lived in the same town (Newmarket, once Exeter), and tradition says they were father and son, but we know little else. We don't know Richard's day of birth or the day he died. Even the location of his grave is lost to time. The same goes for his son Hopestill and Hopestill's wife Katherine. Despite the obstacles, there is still hope that someday we could learn more.

New things about the Cheswills are uncovered every year. Some new record or artifact could be discovered tomorrow that changes everything. We might even find a gravestone. In 2022, a gravestone for one of Wentworth Cheswill's daughters, who did not survive infancy, was recovered in the small plot of land that contains the Cheswill family cemetery. It had been hiding beneath a few inches of dirt for centuries. No one knew it was there.

On another occasion, Richard Alperin, who led the restoration of the Cheswill family cemetery, happened upon another gravestone, that of George Mathis, Wentworth Cheswill's grandson. He found it at a yard sale on Maple Street near Packers Falls, just down the road from where the Cheswills had lived. The homeowner discovered it while rebuilding a collapsed brick walkway. Burial records showed that George Mathis was buried quite a distance away in Newmarket's

Riverside Cemetery. Only recently was the gravestone placed over the boy's final resting place, horizontal, as cemetery rules allow only one vertical headstone for the family.

Perhaps these are grim examples, but it shows that even a bit of home restoration could uncover something related to the Cheswills. Not far from the back entrance to the Cheswill family cemetery, there are three small stones in a line sticking out of the ground. Radar has revealed grave shafts, but who is buried there is unknown. Could Hopestill and his wife be there? What about Richard himself or his mysterious partner Jane? What other clues might be hiding just below the earth? Should we dig them up? As the director for UNH's Center for Humanities, anthropological archeologist Meghan Howey, reminded me during a week-long program I attended in association with the National Endowment for the Humanities: "American archeologists don't exhume graves for research."

Let's get back to Jane.

Glen Knoblock, a prolific scholar you should really check out, has written much about the curiosities of New Hampshire history. He too made the claim that Richard Cheswill had a relationship with a woman named Jane, but let me be clear that there are actually two reputable candidates for Richard's partner, the mother of Hopestill, grandmother to Wentworth Cheswill, and both of them are named Jane Cate. Or Cates. Or Jose. Maybe Vose.

Local historians, including the prolific Janice Brown whose extensive work on the Cheswills you can explore on her New Hampshire history blog *Cow Hampshire*, point to one Jane over the other Jane, but I assure you that I learned a lot more by investigating both women. Research into the identity of Jane reveals a surprising cast of characters and yet another layer of mystery. While one of these two may have been the mother of Hopestill, both teach us about the complexities of life, especially for women, during this time period.

The first candidate is Jane Jose, born July 20, 1689 to Richard Jose Sr. and Hannah Ayres. Jane married Edward Cate Jr. in 1717. This is the same year that Richard bought land from Joseph Hilton, who just so happened to be married to Jane's sister, Hannah. An interesting connection, right? Another potential clue is that Edward Cate Jr. was a housewright, Hopestill's eventual profession. Perhaps Richard didn't raise Hopestill in the wilderness after all. Perhaps the boy lived with his mother, Jane, and learned the trade from his adopted father, Edward.

This would be a closed case if it were not for the other Jane.

The second Jane Cate was born in 1697. She was the daughter of housewright John Cate and Joanna Johnson. This Jane had several children prior to her marriage, including a son named Paul March who has been directly linked to the Cheswills. In Charles W. Brewster's 1873 multi-volume *Rambles about Portsmouth*, Paul March is called a half brother of "Hopestill Caswell." Brewster collected stories from the elders of the community and published a regular column amounting to one hundred and forty-nine essays written over the course of fifty years for the *Portsmouth Journal*. The March family had a memorable reputation in court, and it wasn't a good one. Multiple members of the March family are remembered for abusive and exploitative behavior, including denying children they conceived out of wedlock.

From what I can gather, Paul March's father was one of two men. Both men were known to abandon or deny their children. In Brewster's *Rambles*, he specifically refers to "Hopestill Caswell, a mulatto, a half brother of Paul March." Paul was the illegitimate son of either James March or Clement March Sr. with a woman named, hold onto your seat, Jane Cate. Several members of the March family were in and out of court, facing charges for all manner of despicable actions, from lack of payment for services to drunken brawls and illegitimate children. Jane Cate accused Clement March of fathering her child, also named Clement, which he vehemently denied.

Keep in mind that many of these stories were passed to Charles Brewster orally. The Portsmouth elders he interviewed for his column may or may not have had foggy memories. Regardless, in 1859, Clement March's great-great grandson, also named Clement March (nothing comes easy with this stuff), wrote in his diary that "George Brewster, a brother of the (Portsmouth) Journal man, tells me that Clement March was a son of a woman by the name of Cate, by an unknown father, but claimed to be a son of my great-grandfather who would not own him." The diary entry implies that the earlier Clement March was the sometime partner of Jane Cate. To be clear: I am quoting a circa 1859 diary entry from a guy recounting a rumor about his great grandfather told to him not by Charles Brewster but by his brother George. This is like a historical game of telephone. It is very likely that none of this can be trusted.

To make matters more complex (for me and therefore you), I will add James March to the mix. Rather than Clement March, James may have actually been the father of Paul March. James was known to have kept a halfway house for women, and he was also known to have had several children with the women he housed. He later denied relation to any of the children (even in court), but, in 1717, the very year Jane #1 was married and Richard bought land from her brother-in-law, there was a court case in which James March faced charges "for living with and entertaining those women by whom they had bastard children." Left to care for her own "bastard" child, Jane may have met up with Richard Cheswill only to bear Paul March's half brother Hopestill.

Ultimately James March never admitted to fathering children he almost certainly fathered, but he did marry and have more children after all this went down. His formal attempt at a family did not last though. His wife was shot in the back with an arrow while she was standing at their front door. And all their children died of diphtheria in 1735.

Any archeologist can tell you: people lie, objects don't. Perhaps there is a more substantial clue to the Cheswill family lineage among the impressive structures that Hopestill Cheswill built, some of which still stand today. These immense buildings might contain physical clues that rumors and hearsay cannot provide. The buildings earned Hopestill wealth and influence in a world that might have otherwise rejected him. Perhaps a clue to his origins can be found in his skilled work or maybe there is a traceable technique that was passed to him from the housewright who taught him the craft. Each Jane Cate had intimate access to a housewright. Either had someone in the household who could have taught her son the skills to succeed later in life.

So, who taught Hopestill to frame a house with a gambrel roof?

Hopestill's houses are easily spotted among the other historical buildings that populate Portsmouth because each roof changes in slope partway up. While he was by no means the only builder of gambrel roofs, all of his remaining structures exhibit this noticeable feature. Over in Exeter, the Maj. John Gilman House (not built by Hopestill) is an example of this dynamic design. It was built in 1738 by Colonel John Gilman for his son, also named John. Hopestill was 26 years old when it was built. During this time, the roof type was most commonly attributed to the Dutch. Gambrel roofs are known as Dutch roofs, even today. The once celebrated fireside poet Oliver Wendell Holmes, Sr. wrote in 1858:

> Know old Cambridge? Hope you do.—
> Born there? Don't say so! I was, too.
> (Born in a house with a gambrel-roof,—
> Standing still, if you must have proof.—
> "Gambrel?—Gambrel?"—Let me beg
> You'll look at a horse's hinder leg,—
> First great angle above the hoof,—
> That's the gambrel; hence gambrel-roof.

Each of the Janes I profiled had housewrights in the family, but were any of them Dutch? These are the thoughts that enter my head in the middle of the night. Thankfully (for my sleep) this may be an investigatory dead end. If there was a Dutch building influence in the family, then either household could have benefited, because, final drum roll please, the two Jane Cates were related. The husband of Jane #1 was the first cousin of Jane #2.

The two Janes probably knew each other.

Two related women went by Jane Cate or Cates, both lived in the same region, and both had master housewrights in the family who could have helped Hopestill learn the trade. Either one of these women may have had an affair with Richard Cheswill. Or neither of them did. Charles Brewster (and his brother George) might have confused the two Janes or even the two March men (or some combination of all of them).

For the last few pages, I tried to determine meaning from old tales, traditions, and rumors, hoping they might reveal something about the life of Richard Cheswill, the grandfather of Wentworth Cheswill. Clearly there is something here. In the muddled history, there is an actual story of an unlikely couple surviving in a harsh world. Unfortunately we may never determine the exact details of that story. In many ways, what we know about Richard ended a while back, but it is clear that the extraordinary Cheswill family saga began with him.

Richard and his partner, whoever she was, surely lived harrowing lives. The deeper I dig, the sadder the stories I uncover. If any children survived the various epidemics and brutal winters, then there was still the justifiably enraged indigenous population to contend with. Tired of the settlers reneging on treaties and enslaving their men, women, and children (look up 1676's Cocheco Treaty from nearby Dover), local tribes were fighting back. It was not uncommon for settlers to be killed on their doorsteps in retribution for insincere diplomacy or downright treachery. When the Treaty of Portsmouth was being signed, the Wabanaki Confederacy was still raiding villages including Exeter, as well as nearby Oyster River (Durham), and Dover. Newmarket was right in the middle of it all.

The obstacles Richard Cheswill faced after he was granted his freedom were surely paramount. In the seven years between his gaining freedom and buying land, there were hardships for him that we will never know. Where did he live? How did he survive? Most of his life is mere speculation. Whether his origins were scandalous or mundane, Hopestill, like his father Richard before him, grew into a phenomenon worthy of historical appreciation, even beyond those gambrel roofs.

HOPESTILL CHESWILL

"Hope" is the thing with feathers—
That perches in the soul—
And sings the tune without the words—
And never stops—at all—
                    —Emily Dickinson, Poem 314

Hopestill Cheswill made the most of every opportunity, growing his acerage, buying into mill partnerships, and petitioning to establish roads and bridges that would support economic and community development for generations to come. Hopestill, the son of Richard Cheswill, grew up to be an astonishingly pivotal member of his community.

Through his hard work and sound investment, he was able to provide his son Wentworth with unparalleled opportunities, setting the young man on a path to contribute to the birth of a nation.

Hundreds of years later it is evident that Hopestill lived a dual life.

Mentions of his time in nearby Portsmouth, where he worked framing houses for prominent citizens, directly reference his skin color. Here, he was remembered as a "mulatto" housewright and carpenter, hesitant to approach a house he himself built, for the occasion of a house warming celebration, unless explicitly welcomed in by the owner. Even modern mentions of him, among the websites developed around the houses he built, are quick to reference his race. On the other hand, there are no references to his skin color from the centuries old historical town records of Newmarket, twelve miles away, where he lived, married, and raised a child. Here, it was Hopestill who was the prominent citizen. The housewright seemed to embody the qualities present in his name—in that there was *hope still* for those born out of the tragedy of human enslavement.

In his thesis written in 1995 at the University of New Hampshire, Erik Tuveson directly points to this dichotomy, Hopestill's dual personas, saying, "Hopestill Cheswill prospered from his craft, owned substantial amounts of property, took part in town affairs, and appears to have been accepted and identified as a member of the Newmarket community. It is interesting to note that every deed pertaining to Hopestill Cheswill refers to him as a 'Carpenter' or 'Housewright' living in Newmarket. Not once do the deeds mention his race." Tuveson goes on to say, "However, there is reason to believe that because Hopestill Cheswill was a 'mulatto,' he was not always perceived as an equal, either by himself or by others."

Born free, Hopestill never experienced the level of hardship his father endured, but that terrible institution surely lurked like a specter his entire life. Many mixed race individuals in his community were enslaved. In 1767, when Hopestill was in his mid-fifties, there were 29 enslaved people in Newmarket alone. There were many more in Portsmouth where he worked his trade. He surely knew these people by name while he walked freely among them.

I infer that Hopestill Cheswill worked hard to make sure that no one in his family would ever be enslaved again. For one, he invested in his son Wentworth's education at a remarkable level. Also, much of Hopestill's land would be transferred to his son while the boy was still young. Hopestill seemed to be carrying out a calculated plan to give his son the opportunities that he and his father Richard never experienced. Hopestill's actions enabled a generational leap in education and, in turn, prosperity for the family. Hopestill was the bridge between his father's enslavement and his son's pursuit of the unalienable right to liberty for all.

Like the life of his father, many of the most basic details of Hopestill Cheswill's life are unknown. His day of birth and date of death are a mystery. Both he and his wife Katherine fade from public record, and, even today, Hopestill's accomplishments remain tragically underappreciated.

Hopestill's Portsmouth structures are big, looming three-story mansion houses, meant to be seen and admired. They tower over their visitors, brazen with windows and dual chimneys. While we don't know for certain, it can be inferred that the home Hopestill built for himself in Newmarket was modest in comparison. According to the Boston Club of Newmarket, by the early 1900s all that was left of Hopestill's home was an impression in the ground and a memory.

One of the earliest activities of Hopestill I can trace is when on the day of the winter solstice he bought land from Samuel and Elizabeth Rawlins. It was December 21, 1733, and he would have been around 21 years old. There happens to be an incredible account of Samuel Rawlins and his family written by none other than Wentworth Cheswill. In a letter to clergyman and celebrated historian Jeremy Belknap, Wentworth told a terrifying story that probably came to him by way of his father. An excerpt of the letter was published in the *Salmagundi* journal in 1820. These journals were produced by James Kirke Paulding, a longtime collaborator with Washington Irving. Paulding was also briefly the United States Secretary of the Navy and, like Paul Revere, had a warship named in his honor.

Be forewarned that it is an intense account, and I will be quoting Wentworth Cheswill verbatim:

> The people there at the time commonly retired at night to the garrisoned houses, and returned home in the day time; but that night they neglected to retire as usual. It seems the Indian scout consisted of eighteen, who probably had been reconnoitering some time, and intended to destroy both the families of Aaron and Samuel Rawlins, at the same time. For this purpose they divided, and nine went to each house. But the party that went to Samuel Rawlins's, beating in the

window, and finding the family gone, immediately joined their companions who were engaged at Aaron's. His wife went out of the door, perhaps sooner than they would otherwise have assaulted the house, and was immediately seized with two of her children that followed her. Her husband being alarmed, secured the door before they could enter, and with his eldest daughter, about twelve years old, stood upon the defensive, repeatedly firing whenever they attempted to enter, and at the same time calling earnestly to his neighbours for help. But the people in the several garrisoned houses near, apprehending from the noise and incessant firing, the number of the enemy to be greater than they were, and expecting every moment to be attacked themselves, did not venture to come to his assistance. Having for some time bravely withstood such unequal force, he was at last killed by their random shots, through the house, which they then broke open and killed his daughter. They scalped him, and cut off his daughter's head, either through haste, or probably being enraged against her, on account of the assistance she had afforded her father in their defence, which evidently appeared from her hands being soiled with powder. His wife and two children, a son and a daughter they carried to Canada. The woman was redeemed in a few years. The son was adopted by the Indians, and lived with them all his days. He came into Pennycook with the Indians after the peace, and expressed to some people with whom he conversed, much resentment against his uncle, Samuel Rawlins, supposing he had detained from his mother some property left by his father, but manifested no desire of returning to New Market again. The daughter married with a Frenchman, and when she was near sixty years old, returned with her husband to her native place, in expectation of recovering the patrimony she conceived was left at the death of her father. But the estate having been sold by her grand-father's administrator, they were disappointed, and after a year or two went back to Canada.

Within a month of Hopestill purchasing land from the Rawlins family, one hundred and fifty Africans led by an enslaved woman from Ghana revolted in one of the earliest mass insurrections of the enslaved in the Americas. This event occurred on the island of St. John in what is now the United States Virgin Islands. Meanwhile, back in New Hampshire, Hopestill was free, working, buying land, and building his house on the south side of the Newmarket's Piscassic River.

In 1741, Hopestill purchased land from John Taylor. It was twenty acres out of Edward Hilton's mill grant. Taylor had been severely wounded several decades earlier when twenty indigenous people attacked a group of colonists mowing a field. In the skirmish, four men were killed.

Two years later, Hopestill would buy land from Ephraim Folsom, once owned by his father Ephraim Folsom, who was killed by an indigenous attacker near Crow & Eagle Falls on the Piscassic River back in 1709, the year that Richard Cheswill was freed from enslavement.

The Cheswill family seemed to regularly acquire land from families with recent conflict with the indigenous population, but this may be a statistical fallacy. Rather than the Cheswills taking advantage of these situations, it is more likely that the conflict between the settlers and the indigenous population was pervasive in the years leading up to Hopestill's land acquisitions. The escalating conflict affected everyone.

In 1745, Hopestill built the Marquis of Rockingham (later renamed the Bell Tavern) for Paul March, his alleged half brother. It is notable that the place was named after the Marquis of Rockingham, a member of the Wentworth family of governors. Charles Brewster wrote about the tavern, saying:

That it was strongly made, the test of a century and a quarter has shown. On the completion of the work there was, according to the custom of the day, a merry gathering to commemorate it. Though Hopestill had performed an important part of the work, he did not venture to approach the board, until it was decided by the company that he should be permitted to come in and partake with them on the joyful occasion.

Brewster recounts that Hopestill was a "mulatto" without offering much about the appearance of the others in his *Ramblings*. Could Paul March have employed Hopestill as a way to show the community that his kin was worthy of acceptance? At least to Brewster, Hopestill's race was notable enough to be remembered a hundred years later. His appearance was a defining detail beyond his business sensibilities, land acquisitions, and home construction achievements. The complexity of his social interaction on account of his race was so significant, at least to Brewster's source, that it was worth recounting many decades later.

Nowadays Hopestill's buildings carry all sorts of stories with them. For example, the Bell Tavern boasted a run-in with notorious criminal Henry Tufts whose life is accounted for (and embellished) in his 1807 autobiography, *A Narrative of the Life, Adventures, Travels and Sufferings of Henry Tufts, Now Residing at Lemington, in the District of Maine. In Substance as Compiled from his own Mouth.* We can assume he named the book himself. According to Tufts, he was disarmed in the tavern's lobby by General John Sullivan and Colonel Joseph Cilley after Tufts sought revenge on a couple of soldiers who beat him in the street, knocking some of his teeth out. After a few moments perusing Tuft's autobiography, this event is no surprise. Tufts was a notorious liar. Interestingly, Tufts was born in Newmarket, two years after Wentworth Cheswill. The two men probably did not know each other though. Tufts was raised in the nearby town of Lee.

It is recounted in *On the Road North of Boston: New Hampshire Taverns and Turnpikes, 1700-1900* by Donna-Belle Garvin and James L. Garvin, that the second president of the United States, John Adams, described the Bell Tavern as having, "a spacious Yard, good stables, and an excellent Garden, full of Carrotts, Beets, Cabbages, and Colliflowers-" Who knew President Adams was such an appreciator of vegetables? Unfortunately, we cannot share in his enjoyment because the garden is no longer there. The building is gone too. Like the fate of many of the buildings of the era, the Bell Tavern burned to the ground. It was lost in February of 1867, an event worthy enough for *The New York Times* to mention it.

At some point, Hopestill married Katherine (sometimes recorded as Catherine) Keniston, though we don't know when. In *Black Portsmouth* by Sammons and Cunningham, Hopestill's wife is referred to as "an illiterate white woman." While Hopestill left behind his share of buildings and traditions, we seem to know even less about his wife. Some sources say she was from a well-to-do family from Newmarket or Durham. There were certainly Kenistons around, but they are generally all accounted for. None were named Katherine or Catherine. The spelling of the surname Keniston evolved in those years, so she could have come from any number of the local Kiniston, Kenaston, Keniston, Kyniston, or Kynaston families. The Newmarket Club of Boston believed she was "probably (the) daughter of Christopher (Keniston) who owned a house in Mill Grant." If she was indeed one of Christopher's daughters, then the families would have been curiously close. Christopher had a daughter named Judith Kenniston Crommett. She was the maternal grandmother of Mary Davis, the future wife of Wentworth Cheswill.

After he built the Bell Tavern, Hopestill Cheswill appeared again three years later on a petition to establish a bridge between Newmarket and what would become Stratham. It was 1746, the year of his son Wentworth's birth. At this time, Hopestill and Katherine were comfortably living in Newmarket along the Piscassic River. Hopestill was surely setting his sights on increasing his business opportunities. The bridge he proposed would replace the need for a ferry, which was not up for the demand of the expanding local trade.

A year after that, Hopestill was still involved in shaping the town. His name appeared on another petition. This time he and a neighbor wanted to establish the road that would become South Main Street in Newmarket, where the Cheswill family cemetery and the roadside historical marker now reside. In the coming centuries, Hopestill's road would become the town municipal center. The town hall and the community's two schools are on this road today. All this land was once owned by the Cheswill family. It's a wonder the road is not named after them.

When his son Wentworth was two years old, Hopestill was chosen to be the town constable. The office of constable was one of the earliest offices one could serve in the colonies. The first was appointed in Plymouth Colony in 1632. It is notable that in 1748, the son of a formerly enslaved man was trusted to oversee the enforcement of town rules and community practices. For all intents and purposes, Hopestill was the community's law enforcer.

Now it may occur to you that it says on the cover of this very book (and is oft repeated in articles and online resources about the Cheswills) that Wentworth Cheswill, Hopestill's son, was the first person of African descent elected to public office in the United States of America. This is still the case. Wentworth still seems to be the only person of color to be serving in an elected office at the nation's birth. With that said, it does appear that others, at least his father, were serving in appointed or selected positions much earlier. Whether Hopestill was appointed, selected, or elected is unknown, but his service certainly must have been a reflection of the trust he garnered from the community. He would open the door to other people of color serving in the same role, including his son.

Before I go any further, it is worth mentioning the reason why anyone knows this much about Hopestill Cheswill at all. You see, there was a self appointed town historian a few years later, a scrivener who would mention Hopestill early in his journal of transcribed town records, all of which we still have to this day. The journal in question was more of what is called a commonplace book. This was an information management system of the time, a book that stored notable records and articles transcribed word-for-word by owner. The commonplace book, now kept at the University of New Hampshire, is the earliest recording of Newmarket's town proceedings. The original documents were lost in a fire in 1790. Therefore, this handwritten journal is a veritable treasure of American colonial history. The self appointed town historian and scrivener we can thank for saving these records was none other than Wentworth Cheswill.

Here is an example of a town record Wentworth copied into his commonplace book. It addresses the creation of Newmarket's South Main Street:

> We Joseph Smith and Hopestill Cheswill doth agree to lay open a Way of two Rods wide (each allowing one Rod distant) from the dividing Line betwen us it being that Line that runs down from the place where said Cheswill once had a Gate, and so out to that way that leads from Wadleighs mill to the Lower Landing at Lamper eal River, it being for the use of the publeck. Newmarket June ye 3d 1749.

The original document Wentworth Cheswill transcribed in his journal for safekeeping would have been originally drafted when he was only three years old. The "Lamper eal River" mentioned is of course the Lamprey River, which begins in the Saddleback Mountains of Northwood and meanders forty-nine miles to Newmarket and the Great Bay. The river's name originates with the eel-like fish notable for their toothy sucker-mouths that attach to other fish so they can feed on their bodily fluids. These fish live in the sea but they return to freshwater to spawn (and provide nightmare fuel to anyone happening upon them). Years ago, on the banks of the Lamprey River, a conservation group was showing off one of these parasitic carnivores. My three year old son was entertained.

In addition to these successful petitions, Hopestill's role as constable reflected the trust the community had in him beyond any prejudice. What seemed to matter was that Hopestill was a landowner, a mover and shaker who shaped his environment to serve his needs and the needs of his community. His son Wentworth would surely learn from this and later emulate the community engagement practices of his father. On a daily basis, I personally drive on a road or bridge established by Hopestill Cheswill, even though, as I mentioned, at the time of this writing, not a single road or bridge is named after him or his family.

In 1749, Hopestill built a parsonage for Reverend Samuel Langdon, minister of downtown Portsmouth's North Church. This is the same year that Hopestill and Joseph Smith petitioned for the road in Newmarket. Langdon was a theology scholar and would become a devoted patriot as well as a president of Harvard. The building still stands though it was moved to Sturbridge, Massachusetts and now serves as the administration office of the Sturbridge Village Museum. Its removal to Sturbridge was a notable story in its time. According to the Portsmouth Atheneum's website, "Throughout the spring of 1952, the parsonage was painstakingly dismantled piece by piece. On May 28, 1952, the Portsmouth Herald ran a triptych showing the Langdon house demolition in stages under the caption: Going…Going…Gone!"

By the mid-1700s, Hopestill had acquired over a hundred acres of land. He was engaged in the mill and lumber trade in Newmarket as well as the surrounding towns. In 1749, he acquired part ownership of mill and stream in Durham, and part of fall and mill ownership at Wadleigh's Falls. Increasingly he was able to influence the price of materials needed to fund his trade as a housewright and carpenter.

In 1758, Hopestill built the John Paul Jones House, now home of the Portsmouth Historical Society. The three story, gambrel roofed home was built for Gregory Purcell, his wife Sarah, and their five children. When Gregory died, Sarah offered rooms to boarders. Today it is not called the Purcell House because a certain naval hero stayed there in 1777 (and again in 1781). Therefore the house gets his name instead.

My family spent Veterans Day at the John Paul Jones House last year. Upon entering, I came upon Richard Alperin, who I have mentioned was pivotal in restoring the Cheswill family cemetery. I warmly shook his hand. He was surprised that we had appeared at the same place on the same day, but honestly, for Cheswill fans such as ourselves, there is no better place to be on Veterans Day than the John Paul Jones House, named for the father of the American Navy.

Much has been written about John Paul Jones, but I must share one more thing: Ten years after his final stay in Portsmouth, Jones was dead and laid in a lead coffin (with alcohol) in Paris, only to be lost for generations. The cemetery where he was buried was owned by the royal family, sold by the revolutionary government, and eventually forgotten. His body was rediscovered in 1905 by a US Ambassador who searched for Jones' final resting place for six years—a dedication to investigating obscure history that I can relate to. In 1913 John Paul Jones's body was brought to its permanent resting place in Annapolis, Maryland. Before touring the house on Veterans Day, my daughter, age nine at the time, searched the Internet for the image of John Paul Jones exhumed corpse. I had mistakenly let slip at the dinner table that such an image existed. The centuries-old body was mummy-like but served to appropriately disturb my child who later shaded her eyes from the same creepy photo displayed on the second floor of the John Paul Jones House in Portsmouth. Tourists and nine year olds be warned.

Hopestill built a tavern for French and Indian War veteran James Stoodley in 1761 after Stoodley's previous tavern burnt to the ground. Stoodley's Tavern is now part of Strawbery Banke, a historical village with reenactors of various eras educating visitors about Portsmouth's past. Also, a few scenes in the tavern appear in the 1930's novel *Northwest Passage* by Kenneth Roberts, made into a 1940 movie with Spencer Tracy. This place has its share of stories and famous visitors too. Paul Revere even paid Stoodley's Tavern a visit, an important event I will mention again soon. I taught a filmmaking workshop here for several years. I also taught improvisational acting workshops to the junior historical reenactors on the lawn across the street. This was all before I knew anything about the Cheswill family. Even then, I felt a deep sense of history whenever I entered the building. There was just something about it. I felt the same sensation when walking around the John Paul Jones House. It does not escape me that Hopestill's buildings have been repurposed for the pursuit and appreciation of history. They should therefore have staying power, protection against development—as long as they don't burn. Over the centuries, fire has been the fate of many of these old buildings.

As for the house where Hopestill himself lived, according to the Newmarket Club of Boston, it was nothing more than a depression in the ground by the early 20th century. The club tells us that near the

Piscassic River was a trail called Hope's Path and nearby was a cellar hole which "tradition" claimed was the location of Hopestill Cheswill's house and the birthplace of his son Wentworth. Hope's Path is described as having a gate at one end. The path was originally established by the indigenous. Up river a little ways is where Ephraim Folsom was killed, though, by this time, the indigenous population had moved west and north. The club informs us that Hope's Path, as of 1907 at least, could, "be traced, going through the pastures from a point on the Four Corners road north of the bridge over Piscassic river as the road now goes to the falls in the same river, in Robert G. Bennett's pasture." To locals, even now, much of what you read is understandable. Don't know where Robert Bennett's pasture was? Rest assured it can be found on the old maps. Drive down South Main Street past Grant Road and the Piscassic River. Look to the left. It was there. Hope's Path is a little harder to spot though. There is no access, no signage, and no public knowledge of its significance. Regardless, here is where Wentworth Cheswill was born. Maybe someday there will be a historical marker there too.

As for Hopestill and his wife Katherine, as I said, they faded from history without so much as a gravestone left behind to memorialize either of them. Only recently has Hopestill begun to be recognized for his accomplishments as a pioneering pursuer of the American Dream before the concept existed and the nation had even declared its independence.

WENTWORTH CHESWILL

"Perseverance and Spirit have done Wonders in all ages."
—George Washington, 1776

Beginning as early as 1768, Wentworth Cheswill served in community shaping roles in the town of Newmarket. He continued to serve for close to half a century, right up until his death in 1817. The town and the person are so closely connected that the impact of his quill is still felt today. In addition to the wide range of local offices, from surveyor and selectman to moderator and coroner, he also served in positions that reached well beyond his community, including New Hampshire State Representative and Justice of the Peace for the county. His personal story is riddled with legends, but he is undoubtedly a key to New Hampshire history. He helped inform some of its earliest historians with his archeological work. He is also a gateway to learning about early America from the unique perspective of an 18th century prominent person of color.

Since Newmarket's town records through 1784 were destroyed by fire, Wentworth Cheswill's personal journal holds the earliest known copies of his community's origins. Nowadays Newmarket is regarded as a revitalized mill town, but, during the colonial period, Newmarket was a ship building community. As explained in David Chapman's *A Sketch of Newmarket*:

> Early in its history there was a large amount of ship-building and lumbering carried on; probably more ship-building done at one time at Lamprae River Village (Newmarket) than all other branches of the Piscataqua. Seven vessels, some of them quite large for those times, have been seen on the stocks in process of building one at one time, and twenty-one of all kinds have been built in a single year.

The start to any research of Newmarket's colonial past should begin with the meticulous handwriting of Wentworth Cheswill's journal. Several years ago, I brought my mother-in-law and my ten year old son to view his leather bound, handwritten commonplace book, now kept at the University of New Hampshire.

Access to the archive in UNH's Dimond Library is set up like a waiting room. A variety of comfortable chairs rest near objects of curiosity beneath glass cases. At the desk, I requested the journal, reciting its location: a specific collection from a certain box in a particular folder. The librarian raised an eyebrow at my specificity and perhaps my unorthodox research team. She informed me that there was a strong possibility that my "requested material" may be kept off-site. She also gently offered that my request could take a few days to fulfill. I think she was implying that I should have called ahead. I nodded politely, and then I waited. Our trio meandered around the waiting room, trying out chairs, looking at vintage university paraphernalia. Meanwhile the librarian turned away from her computer and lifted a phone receiver to her face, whispered some words, and put it back down. "It's here," she called to me. Five minutes later Wentworth Cheswill's journal was in front of us.

The first thing Wentworth Cheswill transcribed was Newmarket's Act of Incorporation, composed in 1727 in the final months of the reign of King George I when approximately thirty people from northern Exeter petitioned to establish their own parish. His copy of the original document records the town's boundaries as:

> Beginning at the south side of Majr Nicho Gilman's Farm, next to Exeter Town; beginning at the Salt Water, and from thence to run a West north West Line, Four Miles into the Woods: and from thence to turn a North by East Line, while it comes to Dover Line and so bounding upon Dover Line, east & by South to the Extent of the Towns bounds, and so bounding on the Salt Water, to the Bounds first mentioned.

Newmarket was incorporated during an interesting year. The whole world was on the precipice of change. It was the year Johann Sebastian Bach premiered *St. Matthew Passion*, now regarded as a Baroque era masterpiece. Also, this year Lt. Col. Francisco de Mello Palheta smuggled seeds into Brazil in a bouquet that would one day lead to a coffee empire. This same year Janet Horne was executed, burned at the stake in Dornoch, Scotland. She would be the last person legally executed for witchcraft in the British Isles.

Back in New England, just one month before Newmarket's incorporation, an earthquake shook colonists' homes at around 10 o'clock in the evening. In New Castle, New Hampshire, the church tower bell rang due to the intense vibration of the land. In Boston, notorious Puritan clergyman Cotton Mather described the event as "a horrid rumbling like the noise of many coaches together driving on the paved stones with the utmost rapidity." Two years later, Newmarket's own notorious minister, Reverend John Moody, came to town. For this community, including Wentworth Cheswill, Moody would be an inevitable force to be reckoned with.

EARLY INFLUENCES

Newmarket changed ministers a few times before attracting the recent Harvard graduate, John Moody, in 1729. As the new meeting house was built, parishioners met at the parsonage, which was constructed in 1730 and is still standing today. The year he came to Newmarket, John Moody married Ann Hall, and, in 1731, they had a daughter named Mary. They might have had as many as five other children. The reverend would have a significant influence on the life of Wentworth Cheswill from a very young age. Reverend Moody rooted himself in the position of minister, serving for the next forty-eight years—many of which he was a thorn in Wentworth's side.

According to *Old Newmarket* by Nellie Palmer George, John Moody's contract was a longtime point of contention. Nellie notes that, a decade after Moody was hired, "In 1741 money had dropped to one-fourth its value when this contract was signed. Harmony fled from the parish, and the last thirty years of Rev. John Moody's ministry were years of controversy, petitions, resolutions and demands." There were many other challenges to face as well.

In 1745, the year before Wentworth Cheswill's birth, New Hampshire's provincial government voted that "five hundred pairs of snow shoes and an equal number of moccasins" be made for Exeter and Newmarket inhabitants. The winters that year seemed to have been especially harsh.

The following spring, on April 11, 1746, Hopestill and Katherine Cheswill had their baby boy.

Young Wentworth Cheswill was active in church and town affairs from an early age. As a teenager, he had his own pew in the meeting house. It can be inferred that the relationship between John Moody and Wentworth Cheswill was not always contentious. Moody would have officiated the wedding of Wentworth and his wife, Mary. The two men must have addressed town affairs side-by-side for decades despite the growing ire between the minister and his flock. Eventually there would be protests, schisms, and a prolonged confrontation with town leaders. Wentworth would serve on the committee that negotiated the longtime minister's removal. It must have felt like a betrayal to Moody. I suspect he had taken a special interest in young Wentworth, guiding his religious development and even his education—as we shall soon see.

One of John Moody's primary interests was education, specifically the concept of charity schools. These institutions took marginalized youth, whether newly immigrated, indigenous, or impoverished, and provided them with an education to make them productive contributors to the colonies. In September, 1762, Reverend Moody was chairman of a convention of ministers tasked with deciding on a new location for the Moore Indian Charity School, so it could expand its work to educate (and assimilate) indigenous populations. As chair, he influenced the school's move from Connecticut to New Hampshire, and in 1769 it would become Dartmouth College.

Shortly after the convention, sixteen year old Wentworth Cheswill was sent from the Newmarket parish to pursue his education in the inaugural class of a new residential school in Byfield, Massachusetts. The students would be taught by Reverend John Moody's cousin, Samuel Moody. The school would go on to become one of the oldest and most prestigious preparatory schools in the nation. Now it is the Governor's Academy, but, back then, it was called the Dummer School, established by the will of the late William Dummer, two time Governor of the Province of Massachusetts Bay—whose daughter was one of my unlikely candidates for the role of Wentworth Cheswill's mysterious grandmother.

Wentworth Cheswill was one of the first twenty-eight students enrolled at the Dummer School. He studied reading, writing, arithmetic, Greek, Latin, and even swimming. Many have noted that Wentworth acquired a rare level of education compared to his contemporaries back at home. Why was he granted such an opportunity? We don't know for certain.

While occasionally referred to as the Dummer Charity School, the charity aspect appears to be a misnomer. Hopestill paid for his son's enrollment, his boarding, and his books, revealing just how prominent and successful he had become. According to the school's archivist, Sharon Slater, the earliest documentation, including Dummer's will, never mentions that he intended the institution to be a charity school at all. It's a significant detail, because, for the longest time, I assumed

Wentworth was enrolled because Reverend Moody referred the young man to his cousin as a charity case.

Without a doubt, Samuel Moody had a great influence on Wentworth as well as countless others. After that inaugural class, the school's renown rose quickly. Within several decades, and still under the purview of its original schoolmaster, the Dummer School was Dummer Academy, churning out a quarter of the undergraduate student body at Harvard. The education Wentworth Cheswill received here was not rudimentary. It proved to be revolutionary.

Later, as graduates of the Dummer School rose to prominence, the school attracted more and more young people from around New England. At times, the class size rose to as many as seventy students, all under Samuel Moody's singular oversight. This unique teacher was surely an inspiration for Wentworth Cheswill's eventual passions in education and community leadership. Many of Samuel Moody's students went on to become leaders in both education and community, some of the greatest the colonies ever produced. As Samuel's gravestone explained:

> He left no child to mourn his sudden death, (for he died a Bachelor). Yet his numerous Pupils in the U. States will ever retain a lively sense of the Sociability, Industry, Integrity, and Piety he possessed in an uncommon degree, as well as the disinterested, zealous, faithful and useful manner he discharged the duties of the Academy for 30 years.

Countless stories of the teacher paint the picture of an exceedingly eccentric man, who was also beloved. According to a descendent of one of his students, Francis Atkins, the schoolmaster was "a stout, stalwart man, odd and eccentric; but few teachers have been more revered and beloved by their pupils."

By many accounts, Samuel Moody was also emotionally unstable.

There is a story recounted in *The First Century of Dummer Academy; A Historical Discourse, Delivered at Newbury, Byfield Parish, August 12, 1863* by Nehemiah Cleaveland concerning a visiting dancing instructor from

France. Moody had introduced dancing to the boys, which was surely a sight to see. The schoolmaster and the French dancing teacher were allegedly stuck at a door, both being too polite to pass through the threshold. After some gesturing and shrugging, Moody lost his patience, took the Frenchman by his collar, and threw him.

Another story has Moody face off against an unruly student named Preble, who made the mistake of standing by the woodstove at an inappropriate time. Moody instructed the boy to return to his seat. When Preble refused, Moody took up the stove shovel and went to strike the boy. In another version of the same tale, Moody went ahead and struck a nearby desk with the shovel. In both versions, when the boy did not flinch or even blink, Moody looked the rebellious student dead in the eye, and said, "Preble, you are a hero."

The Moody family was a family of ministers. Like his Newmarket cousin, Samuel preached for a time, but his erratic behavior was regarded as better suited for education. According to *Biographical Sketches of the Moody Family, Embracing Notices of Ten Ministers and Several Laymen from 1633 to 1842,* he was described as having suffered from the same "nervous affection" as some of his relatives. The strain of eccentricity was most notable in his father Joseph Moody, who wore a veil over his face whenever he met with the public. As the story goes, on his deathbed the senior Reverend Moody confessed the veil was due to guilt he kept his whole life. Allegedly he confessed to being the cause of death of a boyhood friend, whom he mistakenly shot and killed in a hunting accident. Handkerchief Moody, as Joseph was later known, provided the inspiration for Nathaniel Hawthorne's short story, *The Minister's Black Veil.* The eccentric Joseph Moody had an equally eccentric son in Samuel, and those that knew them both were not hesitant in comparing the two.

All eccentricity aside, Samuel Moody's influence on Wentworth Cheswill was certainly a positive one. According to a blog post offered by Carl A. Pescosolido Library at the Governor's Academy:

> Master Moody influenced the lives of five hundred and twenty-six young men during his career at Dummer Charity

School, the name changing to Dummer Academy after the school was incorporated in 1782. Many of his young scholars became leading citizens to the New Republic. He was instructor to Senator Rufus King, who was a delegate to the Constitutional Convention in Philadelphia and original signer of the Constitution. He taught Tobias Lear, who became private secretary to President George Washington as well as Samuel Osgood, who was appointed as the first Postmaster General under Washington. Master Moody also instructed the naval hero, Commodore Edward Preble, Commander of the USS Constitution, and Samuel Phillips, the founder of Phillips Academy Andover in 1778.

Yes, there he is. Preble, you're a hero.

The current earliest known mention of Wentworth Cheswill in any form comes from the writings of fellow Dummer School student, Stephen Peabody. He recounted in his diary that he shared sleeping quarters, the same bed, as was the custom, with Moses Hale, Samuel Phillips, and Wentworth Cheswill. This list of academic bedfellows provides a microcosm of the character and stature of this inaugural class. Each of these boys grew up to be a minister or a teacher. Stephen Peabody founded Atkinson Academy, a New Hampshire boarding school notable for being the first coeducational school of its kind. Moses Hale, a minister, died relatively young at the age of 38. His mother was another cousin of the school master, another clue that Wentworth may have been given this educational opportunity due to his teacher's relation to Reverend Moody back in Newmarket. As for the third boy, Samuel Phillips, he was a perhaps the most accomplished of them all. His collected papers from this time include a writing book in which the boy repeatedly wrote "Depart from Evil and do good." This mantra proved a self-fulfilling prophecy as he went on to found Phillips Academy in Andover, was a charter member of the American Academy of Arts and Sciences, and became the fifth Lieutenant Governor of Massachusetts. Both the school Samuel Phillips established and the school established by his benefactor, his uncle John

Phillips, three years later and a bit to the north in Exeter, were notable for being open to educating people of color.

The Dummer School was a starting point for many who would shape early America. John Hancock signed the school's articles of incorporation. The seal of the school was designed by Paul Revere. As for Wentworth Cheswill, his passion for history, education, and community service surely started here. He would be driven by those early passions to the end of his days.

THE EDUCATOR

When Wentworth Cheswill returned home from the Dummer School, he was already positioned to be a prominent Newmarket citizen. Not only was he now one of the most educated people in town, but he was already a significant landowner. It was suggested to me that Wentworth Cheswill might have also been a child prodigy, but it is more likely that the prestige and privilege he had at a young age was the plot of his parents.

When he was only ten years old, Wentworth was accepting land owned by his father Hopestill. This generous level of investment continued for years. By age seventeen, Wentworth owned a pew in the Newmarket Meeting House. By age eighteen, he was heavily involved in town affairs, drawing a plan to end a land controversy between Nathaniel Ames Jr., whose family owned a garrison near the Piscassic River, and the town selectmen. This may be the earliest document we have that was drawn up in Wentworth Cheswill's own hand. I infer this task fell upon him because the other parties may not have had his confident ability in reading and writing, especially when it came to interpreting the law. A testament to Wentworth's handling of the situation, Ames was successfully awarded damages in the laying out of Hall's Mill Road two years later.

Upon returning from the Dummer School, Wentworth Cheswill became a teacher. In fact, he was the first teacher in Newmarket to have his own school house. Prior to this time, the colonists hired private instructors to teach kids in their homes. During Wentworth's earliest years, Nehemiah MacNeal was teaching in Newmarket, but he was passed around from family to family who collectively offered the educator room and board. For this reason, teachers were not always well regarded. This point is best made in Washington Irving's 1820 story *The Legend of Sleepy Hollow.* The town of Sleepy Hollow bullied teacher Ichabod Crane with visions of a headless horseman because he was bookish. He was also eating, drinking, and lodging with whatever family had to take him in. It was simply a hassle having a teacher around. The people of Sleepy Hollow resented Ichabod Crane.

I don't think the Newmarket community treated Wentworth Cheswill like the Sleepy Hollow community treated Ichabod Crane. Wentworth had a house of his own, so he didn't need room and board. Secondly, he taught from a one room schoolhouse built on his own land. Finally, Wentworth's passion for education seemed to authentically inspire others around him. By 1776, the town had split into six districts, each with their own schoolhouse. Wentworth Cheswill even served on the town's inaugural school board.

While we don't know much about Wentworth as a teacher, beyond what we can gather on his role model Samuel Moody, we do know a bit about the inside of his schoolhouse. John F. Chapman, born in 1813, a correspondent to the *Newmarket Advertiser*, wrote of the schoolhouse, saying:

> In the south end of the building was a chimney with a huge fireplace, which held wood logs four feet in length and two feet in diameter. In the south west corner was a cloak room. In front of the desk were eight benches, with an aisle in the center. The seats in the back part were four feet higher than the front.

Wentworth Cheswill's schoolhouse was used for about eighty years before it was moved (not burned) in 1848. Moving old buildings was common at this time. These structures were valuable investments, so moving them around happened quite a bit. There are stories of buildings in Newmarket being moved by teams of oxen. When

Wentworth's schoolhouse had run its course, it was moved closer to the Lamprey River, just down the hill from where it originally stood. There it rested behind (what was at the time of this writing and may still be) Newmarket's American Legion.

A new school house made of brick replaced Wentworth Cheswill's wooden one and that building still remains in place. The tradition of education continued in that spot for another 26 years before yet another school, this one made of stone, was built on nearby Zion Hill. The former brick school became a fire station and is now a mix of commercial and residential space. As for the stone school on Zion Hill, it is now the Stone School Museum, the home of the New Market Historical Society.

As for Wentworth's old one room schoolhouse, it was considered significant enough to be moved, but, after it became infested with vermin, it was burned to the ground.

MARY CHESWILL

On September 13, 1767, when he was 20 years old, Wentworth Cheswill married Mary Davis of Durham. She was 17.

The Davis family had been in the region since the earliest European settlements. In 1695, Mary's great grandfather David Davis built a garrison overlooking the Great Bay. The garrison had replaced an earlier one destroyed during an act of indigenous retaliation a year earlier. According to historian B.B.P. Greene in *Davis-Smith Garrison*, "It stood, as a garrison should, on rising ground, and overlooking Great Bay; so that by land or sea, no foe in birch canoe, or skulking bands in woodland, could make approach..." The description seems to be a bit hyperbolic because David Davis was killed near the second garrison the following year.

The Davis family eventually left their home overlooking the Great Bay and moved inland, transferring ownership to local Captain John Smith (hence the Davis-Smith Garrison), and the Davis family moved to a third garrison built by David Davis's son, also named David Davis, near Packers Falls. The second David Davis also had a son named David Davis (stay with me), who married Elizabeth Crommet. This couple had a daughter, Mary Davis, who would marry Wentworth Cheswill.

As for the original garrison, in 1939, descendents of Wentworth Cheswill and Mary Davis unveiled a memorial marker off of Bay Road where it runs over the site of the corner of the old garrison's buried cellar. The marker is easily seen without getting out of your vehicle. This would be the last recorded public appearance of people self-identifying as Cheswill descendents for more than a half century.

The 1710 home where Mary grew up is still standing on Packers Falls Road. A few years back, the new owners were having a yard sale. I enthusiastically stopped by. The couple got an earful about their house, which now sits just over the Newmarket/Durham townline. In the 18th century, the town line was actually much closer to the Cheswills. Mary is often referred to as a resident of Durham, but the courting couple were just down the road from each other, no more than a few minutes' ride by car or horse.

A former Durham town councilor, Julian Smith, shared with me that the house on Packers Falls Road was where "Wentworth and Mary did their bundling." I thought it was his colloquial way of saying that they dated each other, but he pushed the matter further, asking me if I knew what he meant. I admitted I did not. He explained that it was a courtship tradition, once popular in the New England colonies, though now mostly forgotten. Here are the lurid details: The courting couple shared a bed for the night, fully clothed, separated by a slab of wood known as a bundling board. Despite sleeping together, they were unable to touch each other during the night on account of said board.

Born February 19, 1750, Mary was four years younger than her husband and would go on to live eight years longer than he did. While we do know a lot about her family, we know little about Mary herself. We know she was born to a family who had contributed to the colonies for generations. We know she was part of the same Davis family who owned what is now Wagon Hill Farm, a popular recreational spot in Durham. My family takes walks there and enjoys winter sledding on its eponymous hill. We know that Wentworth and Mary would go on to raise eleven children. Two additional children did not survive infancy.

This matter of a large family is something the community of Newmarket was known for. As described in a *Sketch of New Market*, published in 1872 as part of the town directory:

> One other remarkable fact in regard to said town, is the number of large families of children, each by single or only marriages, especially of the exact number of twelve. The writer has been intimately acquainted with sixteen of such.

The author goes on to list over twenty families, many boasting more than twelve children in their households. The families of Wentworth Cheswill as well as his son Thomas were included. It is likely the author didn't know that Wentworth and Mary had thirteen children with two not surviving infancy. With multiple generations of large families, the Cheswills enjoy a great number of descendants, even today.

The first Cheswill descendent I had the honor of meeting was over breakfast at the International House of Pancakes in Newington, New Hampshire at the invitation of Richard Alperin, who was pivotal in the restoration of the Cheswill family cemetery and the placement of Wentworth Cheswill's historical marker. It was the first time I met him as well. The restaurant was his choice.

As I sat down, Richard explained that the two had heard of me and made contact to investigate whether I was "the real deal." I only knew I would be meeting Richard that morning, though he did say he was bringing a surprise. The surprise was his second guest, a woman who looked eager to meet me. The two whispered between themselves and mysteriously passed me a slip of paper across the table. Their eyes were on me as I read a list of names that started with Richard of Exeter, Hopestill Cheswill, and Wentworth Cheswill. The list ended with the name Krista. I looked up and the woman seated beside Richard Alperin introduced herself as Krista. Every year, I meet more and more descendents, but this first time was a well orchestrated moment that I remember fondly.

Krista's late father had been among those who passionately worked with Richard Alperin to restore the cemetery. Over breakfast, we excitedly shared our interest in everything Cheswill. For me, it was the time when my quirky research hobby was blossoming into something more serious. Connecting with others who shared the same interest confirmed for me that Wentworth Cheswill was someone truly remarkable. Here we were eating pancakes, discussing a relatively unknown man who had died hundreds of years earlier.

Over the years, I have met many others who have discovered their relation to the Cheswills. When Mary Cheswill died in 1829, the *Boston Recorder* reported that she left behind nine living children, forty grandchildren, and twelve great-grandchildren. Many living in Newmarket, or those whose families have been in Newmarket for a long time, more often than not, can trace themselves to the Cheswills.

THE MANSION HOUSE

An article titled "The Mansion House of Wentworth Cheswill" was published in May of 1916 for *Granite Monthly* magazine. It was written by Newmarket historian Nellie Palmer George, who as a child lived in the home of Wentworth Cheswill. Nellie's parents rented the estate from Wentworth's daughter, Martha. Nellie, who passed away in 1939, wrote in detail about the house, its furnishings, the plants and the trees that populated the yard, and even the unique look of its portico.

In 1769, Hopestill had sold one hundred acres of land to his son. It was a year and three months after Wentworth and Mary's wedding date, but, according to Nellie, the mansion house was built two years earlier. There are some clues that Nellie's timeline here is off. I will get to that in a moment. At some point, Wentworth and Mary moved into this admirable estate where, as Nellie described, a balm-of-gilead tree dispelled medicinal buds that were "carefully gathered for the healing of the neighborhood." Nellie's details are so specific that I strongly encourage you to toss this book aside for a moment and seek out her 1916 article. It can be found online, including on the New Market Historical Society website. I'll be here when you get back.

Okay, let's continue.

Nellie Palmer George wrote that Wentworth Cheswill's mansion house was built in 1766, but also that he first lived by Moonlight Bridge. Before I go into why I think Nellie is off about the mansion's year of construction, I want to briefly discuss a feature that is mentioned in any description of the birthplace of Wentworth Cheswill. That would be Moonlight Bridge.

When I was invited to join the New Market Historical Society, I asked if there was any remnant left of Moonlight Bridge. I assumed it no longer existed. Newmarket historian Michael Provost said, "You probably drive over it everyday. It's just past Grant Road on South Main Street." And of course he was right. Whenever I have a question about an old place or person from Newmarket, Michael has the answer.

I drove over Moonlight Bridge regularly, almost every day, never seeing it for what it was. Unless one is looking for it, one might not realize that they are passing over the Piscassic River. The site of the home of Hopestill Cheswill, followed by his son Wentworth and later his grandson Thomas, was beside this bridge, but it continued to be a popular site for generations. Another Newmarket historian, Sylvia Getchell, who had a great interest in old maps, claimed that Moonlight Bridge was once also called Cheswill's Bridge. Despite the lackluster bridge of today, there were no less than four different postcards made that featured it. Something about this small piece of road, no more than forty feet in length, with land owned by the Cheswills on both sides, invoked significant nostalgia for the surrounding community.

A 1905 postcard featured lush trees on two sides of the quaint dirt road. The bridge itself is recognized by its short wooden railing. There were two additional postcards made in 1906 with photographs seemingly taken within minutes of each other. One of the photographs was taken fairly close to the same spot as the one from a year earlier, perhaps a few paces back, as it provides a wider view. In this photo, the trees are budding. It looks like it might have been late Spring. A white horse, standing alert, is harnessed to a buggy. The second 1906 postcard depicts the same exact horse and buggy, except the camera was positioned at the riverbank. The white horse's profile reveals the animal's ears pointing backward, no doubt growing tired of all the postcard modeling.

A fourth postcard featuring Moonlight Bridge was issued in 1910. Also taken from the riverbank, in this one, two men are canoeing near the bridge. The wooden railings are recognizable in design but in better condition, showing that some improvements must have been made. What is most impressive about this water level shot is the stone work beneath the road, no doubt a product of 18th century workmanship with 19th century touch ups. It is very possible that some of those stones were placed by either Hopestill or Wentworth, but none of it can be observed as drivers pass by. I literally drove over this bridge for years without realizing it. The current bridge is so unassuming that drivers might not even realize that there is water passing beneath them.

What is bewildering is that these postcards were produced at all. There were other more picturesque bridges closer to the center of town. For some reason, this one little bridge, that for a time sat beside the home of multiple generations of Cheswills, was something of a touchstone. Now it is all lost to the past, and the narrow stream goes unnoticed. Regardless, someone in town liked the sound of moonlight. Not far from Moonlight Bridge, there is a Moonlight Brook and a Moonlight Drive. Could it have been Wentworth himself or perhaps Hopestill who first appreciated the moonlight here?

Down the road from Moonlight Bridge was the site of Wentworth's second home, the aforementioned mansion house. Nellie described the mansion house of Wentworth Cheswill in loving detail in her essay, but there are also details that lead me to think that the house may have been built earlier and therefore not by Wentworth at all. He wasn't married yet when the mansion house was built. He wasn't even a schoolmaster yet. Also, Nellie's description closely resembles the circa 1740 McClary Homestead of Epsom, New Hampshire. That home was built six years before Wentworth was born.

Did Wentworth Cheswill really build himself a mansion house in the break between graduating from the Dummer School and getting his first job as a schoolmaster? Hopestill could have certainly helped Wentworth construct the home, but the house's description doesn't sound like anything Hopestill would have made. There was certainly no mention of a gambrel roof.

Nellie Palmer George lived in the mansion house until the age of 15. For a decade, her family rented it from Martha, the 10th child of Wentworth and Mary. After that, the house was removed and in its place another was built. A year after its removal, Martha died. We have no other recorded witnesses of the house or knowledge of its history. There are no photographs or postcards. Everything we know comes from one, albeit very detailed 1916 essay, the memories of teenager recounted many tears later.

Mansion houses were not mansions in the contemporary sense of the word. These were Georgian-era colonial homes, no bigger than the colonial style homes that survive today. Examples of this type of construction can be found all over New England, including multiple examples in Newmarket and its surrounding towns. The mansion house of Wentworth Cheswill reads like a standard homestead. It certainly was not a looming sea captain's house like the ones Hopestill built in Portsmouth.

The McClary homestead was built in 1740 by John McClary, who emigrated from Scotland with his family when he was six years old. The two houses, the McClary homestead and the Cheswill mansion house, both boasted a central chimney and the same asymmetrical window placement. In comparison, Hopestill built homes that were symmetrical and featured dual chimneys.

If Hopestill helped frame a house for his son (or taught him to do so), then I figure the home would have had some details reminiscent of his trademarks. It did not. Could Wentworth have built the mansion house himself in 1766? It is possible. There is a deed from the previous year showing his purchase of nine acres of land from Joseph Smith. These nine acres were just a stone's throw away down the road. It is possible that he purchased the land and began building his home there, all while courting his future wife even further down the road.

It is also possible that the house was already there.

The McClary homestead, also described in an 1893 article as a "mansion" house, nails the look and design of Nellie's description almost perfectly. It even has a four-foot hidden brick wall on the front side beneath the clapboards. Nellie described a four-foot stone wall along the front of Cheswill house, which "projected from the house and was topped with a slanting roof not more than two feet wide. This roofed wall seemed a part of the house." Her description of the kitchen and the placement of the huge central chimney is also telling, as center chimneys in New England were most often found in pre-1750 structures. She also described the window placement as not being symmetrical: two windows above and below on one side of the front door; one window above and below on the other side. Some houses built during adult-Wentworth's era looked like this—but many more were built like this twenty to thirty years earlier.

It is not my intention to undermine such a wonderful steward of history. I am merely speculating based on similar nearby construction. For now, I bow to Nellie's words. As penance for any insult, I want to offer a quick correction to a piece that I wrote in honor of Wentworth's 275th birthday for *NH Magazine* called *A Toast to Wentworth Cheswill*. In the essay, I referenced Nellie Palmer George's 1916 essay. She wrote about sitting outside the backdoor of the kitchen as she watched Haley's comet. Here she listened to the adults talk about the tragedy of slavery. Except it wasn't Haley's comet. That was my error. It was the Great Comet of 1861. I was wrong. I bring this up because this whole process of researching and reporting on Wentworth Cheswill has shown me how even a small slip up can become rooted to the story. Surely, this is how we got rumors of an affair with the governor's daughter or that Wentworth Cheswill rode almost hand-in-hand alongside Paul Revere. Whether or not Nellie Palmer George was right or wrong about the date the mansion house was built, there are countless other unfounded aspects of Wentworth Cheswill's story that seem to stick around for no reason. The last thing any historian wants to do is misrepresent history, especially when it concerns a man who was himself so passionate about history. An assumption by a historian can become the next generation's truth. So again, sorry about the comet. To make further amends, I offer another poignant observation of that same comet, the Great Comet of 1861. According to Emily

Holder at Fort Jefferson, Florida, "Its appearance was sublime, as it extended over nearly half of the heavens...many wondered if the world was not coming to an end."

Nellie Palmer George truly loved these old places. She concluded in her essay that, "The mansion house of Wentworth Cheswell and the Colonel Joseph Smith three-story brick house, with its upper and lower piazzas, its terraced lawns and its splendid trees, we should have cherished. They were old landmarks, examples of colonial architecture rarely seen in New England today."

I agree, Nellie. We should have cherished these things.

Nellie was raised to appreciate the past. Her father was a Civil War veteran and a staunch abolitionist who raised money to install the town clock whose bell I rang 275 times to mark the anniversary of Wentworth Cheswill's birth. For the event, I wore a tricorn hat and a Fezziwig costume borrowed from a local theater known for its annual production of *A Christmas Carol*. The costume was anachronistic. I was also masked due to the pandemic, but it all worked out. When I showed some initial concern about ringing the bell downtown so many times, the pastor assured me, sharing that she had once rung the bell at Christmastime until the police told her to stop. It is that kind of community-driven passion I appreciate.

THE COMMUNITY LEADER

In 1768, Wentworth Cheswill was 22 years old and a teacher. That year he was appointed town constable, and according to *The Black Presence in the Era of the American Revolution* by Sydney Kaplan, it was also the year he was made Justice of the Peace for his county. While Wentworth provided legal services, most sources agree that he was properly promoted to Justice of the Peace in 1805. Wentworth continued to serve, whether selected or elected, in various public offices every year of his life (except for 1788) until his death in 1817 at the age of 71. For close to five decades he served his fellow citizens in some capacity.

According to the *Encyclopedia of African American History, 1619-1895* written by Graham Russell Hodges and edited by Paul Finkleman, Wentworth Cheswill was the first person of African ancestry to be elected to office in the United States of America. *Encyclopedia Britannica* repeats this accolade, though it adds the word, "probably." A 2007 *Washington Post* piece entitled *The 'Obama before Obama'* by Kevin Merida gave the illustrious title to John Mercer Langston instead. The oversight of Wentworth Cheswill did not last long though. After the article's error was called out by Finkleman, a clarification was made in a 2008 blog post called *The Real "Obama before Obama"* by Daniel Sauerwein for the *History News Network* in association with George Washington University. In the years since that series of articles and blog posts, Wentworth Cheswill's superlative has firmly stuck. No other candidates have come forward, so it does appear that "probably" Wentworth will retain the title.

Like Wentworth Cheswill, I started teaching when I was 22 years old. At the time, I was living down the street from the site of the old Cheswill mansion house and only three doors down from Cheswill's Store, which I will talk about soon. I wouldn't be married for several years let alone have any children. It is impressive to me that hundreds of years earlier, on the very same road, Wentworth would be married with children and already making a significant impact in his community.

The many elected roles that Wentworth Cheswill served in were diverse and complex. He surely had to confront many matters of conscience, starting with his role as constable. His father before him had been chosen to serve in the same role but he was not the only person of color to do so in Newmarket. In 1743, Pomp, a man enslaved by Newmarket's Samuel Gilman, was chosen as constable as well. It is a curious pattern that this community regularly selected people of color, even those who were enslaved, to serve as their constable. In early America, one of the roles a constable played was as the hunter of individuals attempting to escape their enslavement.

Newmarket was no stranger to those trying to escape their captors. From its earliest census records there is a presence of enslaved men and women. In 1767, the year Wentworth and Mary married, there were twenty-nine people recorded as enslaved in town, including thirteen men and sixteen women. Wentworth was still at the Dummer School when Neptune, a man enslaved by Reverend John Moody, escaped from the parsonage. This is the same household where another enslaved man, Scipio, no doubt named after Publius Cornelius Scipio Africanus, a Ancient Roman general, was killed while lowering a hogshead (a large cask) of cider into the wine cellar. Years later, a second enslaved man by the name of Primas would die in the same place and in the same terrible way.

In response to Neptune's escape, Moody posted a notice in the *New Hampshire Gazette* offering a bounty for his return. It read:

> Ran-away on the sixth Day of March 1763, from his Master John Moody of New-Market, in the Province of New-Hampshire, a negro servant named Neptune, of about 25 Years of age; and near six feet high. He had on when he went away, a light colour'd homespun coat with brass buttons, lin'd with homespun, and a green ratteen jacket, and a new felt hat; his under jaw has been broken, so that he can't open his jaws; and one of his great toes has been cut off. Whoever will take up said runaway and return him to his said Master in New-Market in New-Hampshire, or secure him so that his Master may have him again, shall have the value of Five Dollars, in New Hampshire Old Tenor, Reward, and all Necessary Chargers, by me, John Moody.

Neptune had a broken jaw. He had a missing toe, which Moody notes had been severed. The advertisement is a devastating glimpse at a person of color, age 25, attempting to escape enslavement by one of the most powerful members of the community. Meanwhile, Wentworth Cheswill was attending a residential school, enjoying a privilege unknown to most of his contemporaries. This stark contrast, the lives of two men from the same town, shows the tragic divide between one of ample opportunity and one violently kept from it by enslavement.

Five years after Neptune's escape, Wentworth was constable, one of the first electable positions in many settlements. Whoever was elected or selected to the position carried a trust and a mandate. Responsibilities included maintaining order, managing lost livestock, controlling liquor and gambling, and looking out for fires. Had Neptune escaped five years later than he had, it might have been Wentworth Cheswill himself tasked to hunt him down.

Between his role as an educator and his increased involvement in town and church affairs, the respect and responsibility that Wentworth was given early in his adult life seemed to increase with each year. It was 1770 when he was named the executor of the will of Joseph Judkins, an innholder and deacon of the nearby Congregational Church. Wentworth had been teaching for two years and married for three. His land holdings had increased to one hundred and fourteen acres, and he was a couple years into serving in town roles.

Judkins had ties to the Gilman and Folsom families, both very prominent and influential in the region. Judkins's first wife was Abigail Folsom, the daughter of Ephraim Folsom, whose land on the Piscassic River had been purchased by Hopestill years earlier. Twenty four year old Wentworth Cheswill is described in the will of Deacon Judkins, 87 years old when he died, as "my friend." No one else gets such a warm title. I find this charming.

Upon his death, Deacon Judkins gave the church a silver cup made by Newmarket's William Cario, son of the Boston silversmith, also named William Cario. A photograph of the cup was included in an article that originally appeared in *American Collector* magazine, a publication which ran from 1933-1948 but is available at the time of this writing on the *Collector's Weekly* website. This silver cup may be the only object still existing in the modern era that we can claim was held by both Wentworth Cheswill and Reverend John Moody. With that said, the current location of the cup is unknown. Let me know if you locate it.

It should be noted that a person in their twenties holding public office during colonial times was not unheard of. In fact, it was quite common. What is inspiring is that Wentworth would serve for so many years. Beyond the positions he held, there were also the elections he lost or positions he was elected to and ended up not serving. For example, he served in the state's House of Representatives, but he lost a later bid for the State Senate. Look no further for proof that Wentworth Cheswill earns the title of Newmarket's town father than a list of the positions he held. Nellie Palmer George offered a list of some of his elected offices from 1783 to his death:

> He was a selectman in 1783, '85, and '95; assessor 1784, '86, '87, '91, '97, and '99. auditor 1786, '99, 1801, '04, '12, '14, and '16, coroner 1786, and '87; representative 1801; moderator 1801, '04, '07, '09, '11, '13, and '16.

For historical perspective, the signing of the United States Constitution was on September 17, 1787.

The summary above does not include the various ad-hoc committees and special opportunities during this time period. For example, he was chosen to go to Concord and help draft the New Hampshire constitution in 1784. For unknown reasons, he was unable to attend. He and Mary would lose a child at birth early the next year. Perhaps it had been a rough pregnancy, and Wentworth could not bring himself to leave his wife's side. He was also Justice of the Peace (more like a judge or magistrate in those days) from 1805 until the day he died. Also excluded are the offices he held during his time with the secret order of Freemasonry. Like many men of his era and social stature, Wentworth was involved in the order. The Master Mason degree, which he held, is the highest degree and traditionally honors a man's maturity through increased knowledge and wisdom. Interestingly, Wentworth would quit the group. In fact, he was the first master of Freemasonry to be impeached in New Hampshire.

Over the years, several masons have contacted me inquiring about Wentworth Cheswill's involvement in freemasonry and his mysterious exit. He was charged in late 1804, and he was brought to trial, found guilty, and impeached on the 12th of December of that year. The official ruling was that he be sentenced for an "error of judgement."

According to the *Journal of Proceedings of the M. W. Grand Lodge of the Ancient and Honorable Fraternity of Free and Accepted Masons:*

> No Master, to our knowledge, has been impeached, save for official misconduct. The first instance was that of Wentworth Cheswell (sic), Master of Columbian Lodge. No. 2, who on the second Monday of November, A.L. 5804, was "summoned" to appear before the Grand Lodge on the 12th day of December, A.L. 5804, for trial upon the following article of impeachment: 'Art. 1 Against the W. Master Wentworth Cheswell, for quitting the Chair of Columbian Lodge before a properly qualified brother was elected as his successor, and not opposing that election, and notifying the Grand Lodge of such irregularities.'

So, what was the crime? He quit. That was it. That was the crime.

According to the *Journal*, Wentworth, at the age of 58, stepped down from the Chair of Columbian Lodge in Nottingham, New Hampshire, before his successor could be named. He was brought before the grand lodge, presumably on the third floor of the William Pitt Tavern in Portsmouth. As the lodge's website shares, the room was kept private with grain chaff in the walls and beach sand under the floor to soundproof it. There, he was secretly impeached, though no one would know any of this until many years later.

As mentioned, Wentworth Cheswill is regarded as the first person of African descent elected to public office in the United States. He was certainly serving in elected positions well before and certainly after the Declaration of Independence was distributed. So far, there are no others who can make that claim. Rarely did free people of color serve in elected positions as British subjects prior to the Declaration of Independence, but, after Wentworth Cheswill, people of color did indeed serve. For example, Alexander Lucius Twilight was the first African American elected to serve in a state legislature (Vermont) in 1836—but that was much later. John Mercer Langston, the grandfather of celebrated poet Langston Hughes, was the first African American elected to the United States Congress. He was serving as an elected official as early as 1855 as the town clerk of Brownhelm, Ohio. Like Wentworth Cheswill, John Mercer Langston was born to a mixed race parent and a white English parent.

Until some other discovery, it does appear that Wentowrth will keep his title. While these accolades and firsts are fun, it is undeniable that Wentworth Cheswill was a true phenomenon. He was undeniably prolific in terms of public service. If there was a need in his community, then he was ready to serve, even under threat of death—a line that would soon be crossed as the Revolution began. As Wentworth looked steadfast to the future, helping shape it with wise decisions and thoughtful leadership, he never forgot the past.

THE ARCHEOLOGIST

When I was a senior in high school, a letter was delivered to me by my sixth grade English teacher. The letter, which I still have, was written by an eleven year old me. I argued to myself in cursive script that I must someday become a teacher and writer. Honestly, at the time, I was considering the field of archeology, but ultimately I ended up following my own advice. Little did I know that I would one day put the interests together and write a book on the subject of New Hampshire's first archeologist.

Richard Alperin told me that once he gave a talk on Wentworth Cheswill that was followed by a local archeologist publicly challenging him. Richard had claimed in his presentation that Wentworth was New Hampshire's first archeologist. This proved a controversial statement. The archeologist in the audience argued that no one can explicitly declare him to be the first because no one knows if someone else will come along and take away the title someday. Her reasoning did not make Richard happy, but, when the roadside historical marker went up beside the Cheswill family cemetery, a compromise was made. Wentworth was described as a "pioneering archeologist."

According to *The Archeology of New Hampshire* by David R. Starbuck:

There are several candidates for 'the first archeologist' in New Hampshire, but early figures such as Wentworth Cheswill, Sebastian Griffin, and Samuel Sewall Parker deserve special mention, as do Jeremy Belknap (1792), Chandler Potter (1856), and Frederick Putnam (1873)."

Starbuck goes on to note, "Out of this group of early scholars, Dennis Chesley and Mary Beth McAllister have given Wentworth Cheswill the title of 'New Hampshire's first archeologist' because of an archeological report that Cheswill wrote in about 1790." I read that report and I will quote it directly in just a moment. First, I will make a provocative claim: Not only was Wentworth Cheswill of Newmarket the first archeologist in New Hampshire, but he was among the first archeologists in the nation.

The celebrated father of American archeology is none other than Thomas Jefferson, better known as the principal author of the Declaration of Independence. He earned the title digging into a burial mound on his own property and recounting the experience to French ambassador, François Marbois. Jefferson did not record exactly *when* he dug into the burial mound at Monticello, but historians have suggested several dates. Sources listed on Monticello's website include *Jefferson, War and Peace, 1776 to 1784* written in 1947 by Marie Kimball who claimed that his dig probably occurred prior to 1773. She is the only one to make such an early claim though. With each new study, a later date is suggested. In 1978, in the *Quarterly Bulletin of the Archeological Society of Virginia*, C. G. Holland claimed Jefferson's dig was in "about 1780." In 2002's *Jefferson and Science*, Silvio Bedini offered "around 1782."

The term archeologist was not a common one during the time of Thomas Jefferson and Wentworth Cheswill, but the idea was not a new one. In 1685, Jacob Spon of Lyon first used the word "archaeologia" to name the study of ancient monuments. The first archaeological dig was probably ordered as far back as the rule of Babylonian King Nabonidus around 540 BCE. Despite all that, formal archaeology as a concept and practice with agreed upon standards was not commonly known until the early 19th century. Without a doubt, both men, Thomas Jefferson and Wentworth Cheswill, were ahead of their time.

When, in 1790, Wentworth Cheswill sent details of his archeological findings to Jeremy Belknap, clergyman, historian, and one of the founders of the Massachusetts Historical Society, he provided details that Belknap would use in the third volume of his *History of New Hampshire*. The volume, which quotes Wentworth directly, was published the following year.

Wentworth Cheswill's original letters to Jeremy Belknap no longer exist, but Belknap transcribed their correspondence. Scans of these transcriptions were passed to me by local archeologist Hunter Stetz, who requested them from the Massachusetts Archeological Society. Hunter and I met at the event I hosted celebrating Wentworth Cheswill's 275th birthday. In his letter to Jeremy Belknap, Wentworth Cheswill wrote the following words:

> Near the northeast corner of Newmarket at the head of the tide on the Lamprey River is a piece of flat land which, in the ancient grants of the adjacent land, is reserved for a public landing place by the name of the Old Indian Field in which, in digging a well about 30 years past was found a stratum (or layer) of oyster shells, mussel shells, and clam shells mixed together about 4 or five inches thick at seventeen feet below the surface of the ground. The situation cannot be otherwise accounted for other than by supposing that the earth has been washed down from the higher land adjacent, as there is not the least probability to judge from the situation of the circumjacent land that ever the bed of the river has been changed; which supposition is further strengthened by another ancient relic of the aboriginal - found near the same place about the same time - which was a human skeleton of a large stature which appeared to have been buried in a sitting posture. Nothing remained but the bones which appeared sound & hard, though they had then lain there more than a century. Their

soundness might in some measure be owing to the dryness of the ground, which was sandy.

The meticulous nature of Wentworth's description shows he clearly took this stuff seriously. His passion and respect for what he deemed the "aboriginal" past is also evident. He was describing a discovery that he witnessed 30 years earlier, one that he seems to have been involved in intimately, but he presents the facts almost clinically. In terms of the timing, if he wrote these words in 1790, then the discovery of an "ancient relic of the aboriginal" would have occurred in approximately 1760 when Wentworth was fourteen years old.

Earlier I made the claim that his time at the Dummer School was the catalyst that inspired Wentworth's lifelong passion for history, but he might have suggested otherwise in this letter to Jeremy Belknap. Exploring the shell midden and a large skeleton surely contributed to his interest. Even as a boy, he showed deep respect for what was left behind by the Squamscott people who lived in his region prior to the European settlement.

Though he recounted a find that predated Thomas Jefferson's efforts by decades, Wentworth Cheswill was not claiming in this letter that he was the one doing the digging. He was simply reporting on what was found and what he observed as a young adult with eyes of wonder. The second part of his letter provides a look at how the adult Wentworth continued to involve himself in these pursuits. In it, he wrote:

> A similar instance I observed about 15 years past, being on a Journey near Ossipee Pond, I was told by one of the inhabitants there that he had lately observed the appearance of graves in the woods. I had the curiosity to see the place, a small pitch pine knoll in a kind of intervale land, and upon digging found the bones about 2 feet underground buried with the face downwards, the bones all sound of a brownish colour, the teeth also exceeding white & sound &

they remained in the same state after being exposed to the air for several years.

If Wentworth Cheswill wrote this letter to Jeremy Belknap in 1790, then he was recounting an excavation he engaged in around 1775. This would make Wentworth a contender for the earliest archeologist in the nation—with all due respect to Thomas Jefferson.

Last summer I participated in a National Endowment for the Humanities Summer Institute. During the program, I wondered what the archeologists I met would think of the suggestion that Wentworth Cheswill was the first New Hampshire archeologist. He had dug up graves. This is forbidden for modern American archeologists. The fact that Wentworth took measurements is what made his efforts noteworthy. He also thoughtfully interpreted the findings.

In the account Wentworth sent about the burials near Ossipee Pond, there is a phrase that Jeremy Belknap struck. How it reads now implies that the indigenous people were buried by their own people. Wentworth's original correspondence offered a different conclusion. He originally stated that, "I was told by one of the Inhabitants there that he had lately observed the appearance of Graves in the woods, and conjectured that they ought be the 10 Indians killed by Capt Lovell about the year 1725." The end of that sentence was struck by Belknap in his journal. Wentworth's interpretation never made it to the *History of New Hampshire*, even though he specifically included that a local believed the site was proof of a terrible moment from history. For whatever reason, Jeremy Belknap felt it improper to include Wentworth's mention of Captain John Lovewell of Dunstable, one of the most infamous scalp hunters of the early eighteenth century.

After Massachusetts declared war on the local tribes, one hundred pounds was offered for every indigenous scalp presented to a magistrate. According to *Military History of New Hampshire* 1623 to 1861 by Chandler Eastman Potter:

> Capt. Lovewell soon found himself at the head of eighty-seven men, and crossed the Merrimack at Dunstable

on the 29th day of January, 1725, on his way to "the Pigwacket country." At the eastward of Lake Winnepesaukee, on the 20th of February, the trail of a party of Indians was discovered, and early in the morning of the following day the Indians were attacked as they were "asleep around a large fire," and the entire party, ten in number, slain. The company proceeded to Boston by the way of Dover, and received their bounty of £1000 from the treasury.

Wentworth Cheswill reported that the remains he investigated may have been connected to this grim act of mass murder. He dug into the ground, measured, and interpreted his findings. Whether or not he was the first archeologist in New Hampshire or merely a pioneering one, his findings were worthy enough to be quoted in the first history of New Hampshire, even if his words were edited a bit.

Captain Lovewell would ultimately fall at the Battle of Pequawket, known as Lovewell's Fight, when he faced Chief Paugus, leader of the Abenaki, face to face, in what is now Fryeburg, Maine. This final battle would be celebrated in songs and stories. More than one hundred years later, poet Henry Wadsworth Longfellow of *Paul Revere's Ride* fame, would immortalize the whole tragedy in another poem, *The Battle of Lovell's Pond*, published three years after Wentworth Cheswill's death.

THE PATRIOT

In the lead up to the War, King George III said of the unruly colonists: "We must either master them or totally leave them to themselves." The British monarchy had fairly diminished powers at this point. The parliament was the main instigator leading up to the Revolution. While the monarchy often gets the blame, the Stamp Act, for example, which greatly inspired the slide towards rebellion, was something the king himself thought was absurd. Regardless, there was no doubt, on either side, that conflict was on the way.

While Henry Wadsworth Longfellow's *Paul Revere's Ride* embellished a great deal, there are some bits it got right. On the evening of April 18, 1775, Paul Revere did spread the word that British regulars were coming to raid the Provincial Congress' stockpile of arms. While he did not ride alone or hang lanterns in the Old North Church like the poem would claim, he absolutely did ride. We know this for certain. He submitted a bill for his efforts. The alarm culminated with the "shot heard 'round the world" when colonists confronted British soldiers in the battles at Lexington and Concord. The start of the war was even recorded in Wentworth Cheswill's journal. In fact, one of the final entries in his commonplace book was: "War commenced 19th April 1775."

Except there was another battle we should all consider.

Four months earlier an event happened that some historians claim to be the actual start of the Revolution. It is the 1774 raid on Fort William and Mary off the coast of New Hampshire. Here, hundreds of colonists committed treason on a wintry Wednesday, the 14th of December.

It is possible Wentworth Cheswill was there.

Here's how it went down: On the day before the raid, a messenger for the Committee of Safety rode into Market Square in downtown Portsmouth, disembarked from his horse, and immediately recognized a man named William Torrey. The messenger demanded Torrey connect him with a man named Samuel Cutts. Torrey and others took the rider immediately to Stoodley's Tavern (built by Hopestill Cheswill) where he would reveal the message that two British warships were coming to secure the powder to prevent it from falling into the hands of the unruly colonists. Local patriots (now revolutionaries) were compelled to act and secure the munitions, leading directly to a raid on the fort.

Like the famed battles at Lexington and Concord, the raid on Fort William and Mary was inspired by a messenger who rode night and day, endangering his life to bring news that the British soldiers were coming. Unlike the glorified ride depicted in Henry Wadsworth Longfellow's poem, this earlier ride has been ignored by the likes of poets and scholars who continue to look to the later battles as the start of the Revolution. In fact, the raid itself is often no more than a footnote outside of New Hampshire. The patriot who delivered the fateful message that kicked off the rebellion that led to the Revolutionary War was not Wentworth Cheswill, but I should at least mention his name lest we forget the man whose ride kicked off this important historical event.

The rider's name was Paul Revere.

Yes, it is true. Several months prior to making his famous (but mostly embellished) ride to kick off the American Revolution, Paul Revere risked his life in a ride that kicked off the American Revolution. History is fun, isn't it?

In the preface to this book, I made the claim that we only know about Paul Revere because of the poem. If it wasn't for the poem by Henry Wadsworth Longfellow, then he might only be known only for failure. The irony is that the brigadier general instrumental in planning the embarrassing Penobscot battle was none other than Peleg Wadsworth, poet Henry Wadsworth Longfellow's grandfather. Hold on. It gets worse. It was Peleg himself who filed the Courts-Martial against Paul Revere with charges of insubordination and cowardice, but Peleg never actually pursued those challenges. It was Paul Revere who had to push for a trial to clear his own name.

One can only wonder if the poet knew what his grandfather had done to poor Paul Revere's reputation and therefore aimed to correct the injustice, albeit two generations later in a poem.

What if I told you that the revolution was not started by the "shot heard 'round the world," but by a long iron bar that now rests in a glass case in the Stone School Museum in Newmarket, New Hampshire?

Historian Joseph Harvey wrote in *An Uncharted Town*, his 1908 article for the *Granite Monthly*, "(It is) a matter of surprise and regret that no adequate record has ever been compiled of (Newmarket), which early in the history of our state and nation played no small part." The raid on Fort William and Mary was led by Portsmouth's John Langdon. He led colonists, including citizens of Newmarket, across frigid, choppy waters for a treasonous raid on King George III's store of munitions. The patriots broke into the fort, allegedly with an iron bar, and, despite violent resistance from the British soldiers, almost a hundred barrels of gunpowder were removed. The colonists ultimately hid the powder throughout the countryside, including Newmarket. The next day a second wave of men, John Sullivan of Durham and Newmarket militia members among them, went to the fort and cleaned out whatever was left behind. They also tore down England's flag.

Both Langdon and Sullivan would go on to be Revolutionary War generals. Both later also served as New Hampshire governors. Also present for the raid was Newmarket's Thomas Tash. In fact, he is the one who took possession of the aforementioned iron bar, which was passed down through several generations of Tash (and eventually Walker) family members until Lloyd Walker donated it to the Stone School Museum in Newmarket in 1971. America's Crowbar, which I have decided to call it, is 35 lbs and is 2/3rds the length of what it once was because the crowbar broke while being employed on a farm after the War. Recently, when I was a guest speaker in my daughter's fifth grade class, I told the story of Wentworth Cheswill but also got to tell them about "America's Crow Bar." I encouraged them to visit the museum and ask for the crowbar by name. Wouldn't it be fun if the nickname stuck?

So, was Wentworth Cheswill at the raid on Fort William and Mary? It is likely but by no means a certainty. After the raid, Wentworth closely worked among those confirmed to be present. Thomas Tash and Wentworth Cheswill had worked together during the lead up to the war as well as members of the Committee of Safety. Like Paul Revere, Wentworth served as a messenger, riding between Newmarket and Exeter, the provincial capital. Ultimately, Wentworth's presence at the raid is a legend that has stuck with him, but, unlike some of the other rumors that follow him, this one is more likely.

Wentworth is recorded as building rafts to support the cause of protecting Portsmouth Harbor and the Piscataqua River. Later, he would be hand selected by John Langdon to join his elite company of soldiers at the battles of Saratoga. Clearly the two men knew each other as trusted patriots. It is possible they participated together in the earlier raid.

In the lead up to the war, Wentworth Cheswill had been engaged in meetings in support of the patriot cause. Things had been heating up ever since the Boston Port Act was passed in March of 1774. A month and a half before the raid, on All Hallows' Eve, voters gathered with Reverend John Moody in the meeting house to decide on how to support the besieged citizens of Boston. Ultimately they voted on a donation of $300. The money was offered after the busy Boston port was closed from trade and its citizens were ordered to financially shoulder the expense of the tea ruined during the Boston Tea Party.

The whole year was a back and forth of increasing tensions culminating in the First Continental Congress's declaration of the Continental Association, a boycott of all British goods. Powder alarms like the one at Fort William and Mary would follow. This "alarm" system was a system of communication that included messenger riders and militia organized into companies called Minutemen, in that they could react at a moment's notice if the royal government tried to take the gunpowder out of the reach of the colonists.

On that All Hallow's Eve in Newmarket, its citizens established formal Committees of Safety and Correspondence. Thomas Tash was chosen Chairman of the Newmarket Committee of Safety. Wentworth Cheswill, age twenty-eight, was voted to be the messenger rider—just like his contemporary Paul Revere. As word of the battles of Lexington and Concord spread through the colonies, it would be Wentworth who would ride to get orders for the local response.

It is this time period that inspired a lot of Wentwoth Cheswill's early 20th century folk hero status. Recounting this time, historian Joseph Harvey wrote of Wentworth Cheswill in the time just before the Revolution in his 1908 essay, *Newmarket on the Lamprey*. In it, he borrows directly from *Paul Revere's Ride*:

> Picture if you can the intensity of the excitement which on that day prevailed in "Mr. Moody's meeting house." Undoubtedly at the door stood Cheswell's horse and he,

"booted and spurred" for a heavy ride like the immortal Paul Revere, "springs to the saddle, the bridle he turns, but lingers and gazes till—" the vote of the meeting is announced, then bending forward, with word and spur, he urges the faithful beast to highest speed.

The poetic pageantry was undeniable. Wentworth Cheswill was a folk hero to be remembered for all ages. Harvey would lay it on even thicker recounting how Wentworth no doubt pondered the coming War as he rode across the countryside:

Remember that the road to Exeter of today is a very different highway from the path which the faithful animal traversed on that October morn, and as the autumn leaves fell thick and fast about his rider's path, he doubtless read in their crimson color a prophecy of the precious blood which, all too soon, would mark the pathway of the colony, but he faltered not, for in two short hours we find him ready to report…"

In her 1932 publication, *Old Newmarket, New Hampshire; historical sketches*, Nellie Palmer George offered her own detailed account of the start of war. She wrote, "On April 21, 1775, the news of the battle of Lexington had reached Newmarket, and a special town meeting was immediately called. It was voted to send thirty men, under the command of Captain Samuel Gilman, to the relief of the Colonies against the regulars, and that each man be paid and billeted against the town." Three days later, another special town meeting was held. According to Nellie, 43 men of Newmarket were enlisted as Minute Men, "completely equipped and ready to march at a minute's notice." In addition, they voted for 24 men "be kept for the safety of the town; that sentinels be kept at the Lamprey River bridge and at the bridge over Exeter River."

As Newmarket's messenger, Wentworth Cheswill carried news back and forth, from Newmarket to Exeter and back. He would return with word on the escalating events to the south.

On the seventeenth of May, 1775, the committee of safety voted that several men, including Captain William Torry, presumably not William Torrey of Portsmouth who met Paul Revere in Market Square, be placed under house arrest. Why was he arrested? William Torry of Newmarket was suspected of being a Tory, a political conservative. The Tory ethos was God, King, and Country, and, in the coming days, more Newmarket men were confined to their homes; some were even jailed. Others were driven from town. A few were kicked out of the state. It was Wentworth Cheswill would have delivered this devastating news. As Joseph Harvey explained in 1908:

> These were days vital with events of gravest importance, not only to the people of this town and the colony of which they were a part, but of the world.

During these tumultuous meetings in Newmarket, voting by a hand count became increasingly difficult. The moderator started asking that those voting "yea" move to the central door of the meeting house. The "nays" needed to move to the women's gallery, which was refused. Nellie Palmer George notes that the moderator must have "had in mind a plan to put the negative voters in an embarrassing position" by putting them in the "squaw seats." She concluded that according to these dissenters, "The women's gallery was no place for a man."

Wentworth Cheswill's name appears on a record dated October 22, 1775, listing the men who contributed to the building of five rafts. It was part of a well documented effort to defend Portsmouth Harbor and "prevent the passage of Enemy's ships up the River…" Others on the list include Wentworth's business partner Benjamin Mead as well as Thomas Tash, eventual keeper of America's Crow Bar.

Incidentally, Thomas Tash would go on to fight in multiple major battles during the Revolutionary War, and, through it all, an enslaved man, Oxford Tash, fought at his side. Oxford's life represents another example of the disparate lives people of color lived in Newmarket during this time period. Wentworth Cheswill would fight as well, but he fought in an elite company known for, I kid you not, its silk stockings.

According to *Historically Speaking: The life and times of Oxford Tash* by Barbara Rimkunas of the Exeter Historical Society, "(Oxford) was a seasoned soldier by 1777 when he re-enlisted in Massachusetts, serving until the end of the war. He saw service at Ticonderoga, White Plains, Monmouth. He suffered smallpox and was, at some point, struck by a musket ball in the thigh." While Wentworth Cheswill was a free man risking his life fighting for freedom for all. Oxford Tash fought as an enslaved man, only earning his freedom after he was discharged from the military. On February 25, 1781, Oxford started a new life. He married, moved to Exeter, and had eight children.

John Carmichael, New Market Historical Society president, shared with me that despite all his suffering due to his wartime injuries, Oxford Tash refused a soldier's pension. I sincerely wonder why. It sounds like he deserved it. After the death of their father, Oxford's children petitioned for their mother to receive a widow's pension, which was granted.

Talk about another guy who deserves to be remembered.

THE SOLDIER

It took just over two weeks for news of the signing of the Declaration of Independence to reach Newmarket. The original draft had denounced the slave trade, but the version that was signed and distributed omitted that bit. I have often wondered what Wentworth might have thought if he knew about this in particular.

Thomas Jeffferson's original Declaration called the enslavement of humans "execrable commerce." He called it "this assemblage of horrors" and a "cruel war against human nature itself, violating its most sacred rights of life & liberties." Jefferson blamed the practice of enslavement in the colonies directly on the king, whom he accused of "captivating & carrying them into slavery in another hemisphere or to incur miserable death in their transportation thither."

If any of these words remained in the Declaration, then perhaps the trajectory of the country towards liberty and equality would have followed a clearer path. Instead it would take a hundred years and a Civil War to begin to correct that cruel and tragic misstep leaving families enslaved in the country for generations.

The original 168-word condemnation of slavery in the Declaration of Independence might have had significant ramifications on a global scale, but, after it was edited out, even Jefferson himself was silent about it. We don't know what he or the other Founding Fathers thought about the removal of those words. Historians have inferred that a critical part of the survival of the colonial economy would be its reliance on Southern plantations, which in turn only survived due to the free labor accrued through the continued practice of human enslavement. Jefferson, later in life, blamed the colonies of South Carolina and Georgia in particular for the devastating edit that continued a blind eye toward the practice of slavery, but he never pushed the matter any further.

What did Wentworth Cheswill think of the Declaration of Independence? What did he think about the references to freedom and liberty, knowing full well of his family's history? Despite being the grandson of a formerly enslaved man living in a community where men and women were still enslaved, he was unabashedly for the patriot cause. This is all we know.

In July, Wentworth Cheswill signed the Association Test of 1776, which was a way to pressure colonists to take a stand for-or-against the cause of independence. As the document decreed, "We the Subscribers, do hereby solemnly engage, and promise, that we will, to the utmost of our Power, at the Risque of our Lives and Fortunes, with Arms, oppose the hostile Proceedings of the British Fleets, and Armies, against the United American Colonies." Not signing the document was a cause for public ridicule. Signing the document was treason. Wentworth signed. He is regarded as one of only two people of color to do so.

Meanwhile, through all of this, Wentworth Cheswill was still engaged in the issues of his community. His passion for education had not abated, and he was selected that year, 1776, to work on a new committee to regulate schooling in town: Newmarket's inaugural school board. Also, by 1776, the long history of complaints about longtime minister John Moody had reached its boiling point. Wentworth would serve as clerk of the committee for Moody's dismissal the following year, which was, by all accounts, an ugly affair. The staunch colonial minister had served the town in his role for decades. Many of the most important meetings, including those involving Newmarket's response to the War, occurred with Moody ever-present. Ultimately, from April 28 to June 13, 1777, Wentworth and others would meet and debate the terms by which the then-72 year old minister would be removed, so as to make way for a new era.

But first, Wentworth Cheswill would go to war under the command of John Langdon.

At the cross section of early American history and New Hampshire history, no one deserves more mention than John Langdon. To truly understand Wentworth Cheswill's position in the fight, one must learn of Langdon, who started as a quiet sea captain but became a dynamic politician who contributed greatly as a founding father. John Langdon's ties with Wentworth Cheswill will be the focus here, but you would benefit from reading more on Langdon himself. Remember that he led the raid on Fort William and Mary. He was also a member of the Second Continental Congress. It is not an exaggeration to say that John Langdon personally bankrolled the New Hampshire Militia at the start of the Revolutionary War. But that's not all. He also oversaw the organization of the Continental Navy, signed the U.S. Constitution, and served as New Hampshire's governor. This still only scratches the surface.

Born to a farmer and shipbuilder from Cornwall, John Langdon rose to become one of New Hampshire's wealthiest citizens. He spent his early twenties as captain of the ship *Andromache* sailing to the West Indies, but, over time, he grew a small fleet of ships that sailed between Portsmouth, the Caribbean islands, and London. When the British government began to mess with the ports and regulate shipping, Langdon turned to rebellion.

Rebellion was the crossroad that brought the two men together.

I can only speculate whether John Langdon and Wentworth Cheswill knew each other prior to the raid on Fort William and Mary, but, later, when Langdon formed his personal company of elite soldiers, handpicked from the New Hampshire militia, Private Wentworth Cheswill was on the roster.

Despite being teased for the silk stockings (paid for by Langdon himself), the group of wealthy and prominent men that served with his personal company were also known to be highly trained and effective. Langdon put a lot of his own money into New Hampshire's forces, going so far as to say, "If we defend our homes and our firesides, I may get my pay; if we do not defend them, the property will be of no value to me."

Suffice to say, Langdon's investment paid off.

Brought together on July 21, 1777, Langdon's Company of Light Horse Volunteers joined John Stark's Brigade and rode the 250 miles to Saratoga, New York, to participate in the first major victory of the revolution for the patriots. Langdon's company, Wentworth Cheswill among them, helped cut off British General John Burgoyne and the rest of the British soldiers from retreat after the pivotal Battle of Freeman's Farm.

The British strategy at the time was to cut off New England from the other states. George Washington was focused on the British forces to the south, so Burgoyne had come down from Canada and captured Fort Ticonderoga. This put New Hampshire's frontier into play. John Stark led the charge in defense at Bennington, Vermont, but, by autumn, Burgoyne's forces had made it as far as Saratoga. There the advance stalled and militia units were called up to help drive him back. John Langdon, Wentworth Cheswill, and the rest arrived and helped surround and overwhelm the British, effectively cutting off their retreat to Canada.

Wentworth Cheswill's close connection to John Langdon produces some interesting possibilities. Over the years, those possibilities have turned to legend. For example, John Langdon was known to have arrived late to the Constitutional Convention in 1787. New Hampshire would not fund delegates' travel to Philadelphia, so Langdon paid the way for himself and the second New Hampshire delegate, Nicholas Gilman of Exeter. The two arrived on July 23. I only bring this up because a rumor has popped up repeatedly in my research that Wentworth Cheswill also traveled to Philadelphia that year—as part of John Langdon's entourage. The following year Wentworth would not serve in an elected position, free of public service for a whole election cycle, something he only allowed himself to do once, and only once, in forty-nine years. Why would a man so dedicated to public service have a single year in five decades when he served in no public office at all? Could it be because he wasn't physically present in New Hampshire to run for office? Could he have been following a greater calling?

Not only has it been repeatedly suggested to me that Wentworth Cheswill didn't run for office that year because he was with John Langdon at the Constitutional Convention, but there are those who have gone so far as to claim he influenced John Landgon's thoughts on the separation of church and state in his recounting of the stresses of the Newmarket's recent religious schisms and the removal of Reverend John Moody from the pulpit. Of course there is no proof of any of this, but remember that folk heroes are surrounded by legend. This is yet another example of the sort of tale that follows our would-be folk hero.

Before I move on, I want to offer two more Wentworth Cheswill legends concerning John Langdon. Both legends also involve President George Washington.

Years after the war, on All Hallow's Eve in 1789, George Washington paid a visit to John Langdon at his home in Portsmouth. It was during a multi-state tour which was intended to unite the new country at the peak of Washington's popularity. The visit was recounted wonderfully by historian J. Dennis Robinson in columns for the *Portsmouth Herald*. I encourage readers to seek out his work.

During the visit, George Washington visited both Portsmouth and Exeter. He fished, attended church, and spent time in taverns. He also honored war veterans. This is the first legend: Wentworth Cheswill was among the soldiers presented to President George Washington during his 1789 tour stop.

As it was told to me, Wentworth Cheswill was witness to President Washington's visit to a tavern in Exeter along with other local veterans. It is notable that Washington did make a brief stop at the Folsom Tavern in Exeter during that grand tour.

Now to the second legend: As a story, the second legend is as unsubstantiated as the first, but it does also involve both George Washington and John Langdon so I am inspired to tell it. While John Langdon did not appear to have trafficked enslaved people during his lifetime, George Washington did. Among the enslaved in the Washington household was a bi-racial woman named Betty. She had a daughter, Ona Judge, who went by Oney, with a white indentured servant. In this way, Ona Judge's mixed racial background was similar to that of Wentworth Cheswill. The Washingtons were known to move enslaved people across state lines in Pennsylvania every six months to avoid Pennsylvania's gradual abolishment law. If they did not traffick their enslaved people across state lines regularly, then they would have had to free them. Their cruel efforts proved useless when Ona Judge escaped from the Washingtons' Philadelphia house.

Ona fled all the way to Portsmouth, New Hampshire.

The escape of Ona Judge would have been smooth if, in Portsmouth, she did not walk past John Langdon's daughter, Elizabeth. The girl recognized the fleeing girl from the previous visit with the Washingtons at her home during that grand tour. News of the sighting made its way back to Philadelphia, and, after several other attempts at retrieving her, Burwell Bassett Jr, Martha Washington's nephew, was sent to New Hampshire to discreetly retrieve the escapee on behalf of the family.

In 1798, Bassett stayed at the Langdon house and ate at the Langdon table, where he openly laid out his plan to kidnap Ona Judge and enslave her once again. Ultimately the plan was unsuccessful, because Ona was warned of the plan, allegedly through the decision of John Langdon himself.

Again, Ona Judge, like Wentworth Cheswill, was the child of a bi-racial and white English parent respectively, but they were people of color living very different lives among the same circles of people. Who or what may have inspired John Langdon to save Ona Judge from her enslavers, two of the most venerated individuals in the history of the United States of America, George and Martha Washington? John Langdon even redesigned a room in his home to pay tribute to Washington. What possessed him to go against his hero? Perhaps he was inspired by a man of color he spent time fighting alongside during the Revolution. At least that is the legend.

Despite John Langdon's influence on early New Hampshire and the very establishment of the United States of America, he himself did not get a call for a statue until a 1915 joint resolution of the New Hampshire State Senate. Unfortunately the resolution didn't go anywhere. There is no statue of Langdon in New Hampshire even to this day, but, in 2015, a life size bronze statue of John Langdon was installed in Signer's Hall at the National Constitution Museum in Philadelphia, the very city Ona Judge escaped from.

As for our folk hero, Wentworth Cheswill served under John Langdon until October 31, 1777. All Hallow's Eve once again, as it has done so many times, appears in the story of Wentworth Cheswill.

THE BUSINESSMAN

Some of Wentworth Cheswill's busiest years were those after the war when he seemed to throw himself into community affairs even more so than when he was younger. While it is wonderful to admire him for his public service, we should not forget that he was also a successful businessman. Beside Wentworth's one room schoolhouse was a store he co-owned. The building still stands, graced by a bronze plaque that reads: Cheswell's Store.

The land in this part of town was once owned by Joseph Smith, son of Captain John Smith, who took on the Smith-Davis Garrison after David Davis was killed. Nearby, where Newmarket's Catholic Church now stands, there was a three story brick garrison. Nellie Palmer George wrote in *Old Newmarket* that, "While this house was building there were rumors of raiding Indians, and to hasten the work the women of the neighborhood put on stout leather aprons and carried the bricks from the yard to the building. Many years later this house was owned by Mead and Cheswell." That would be Benjamin Mead.

After the death of Joseph Smith, his son, also named Joseph Smith, sold the garrison to Benjamin Mead. Wentworth Cheswill and Benjamin Mead, as joint owners, established the small storefront. Like the schoolhouse, the store was eventually moved (in 1849), but, unlike the schoolhouse, it escaped the fate of flames and still remains on South Main Street to this day.

Cheswill's Store is closely nestled between other buildings. It sits diagonally across the street from its original location. Directly across the street is the Tiger #1 engine house, a small fire station built in 1853. It feels good to write all that in the present tense. Nellie Palmer George would be happy to know that all these buildings are still around, though last year Cheswill's Store was graffitied, a true rarity in this town. I have not seen much graffiti anywhere else, but the building is currently office space for a drug testing company. Perhaps that detail inspired the street artist. While there was no fire, the defacement was a sad moment for a building that Newmarket historian Sylvia Getchell once called "one of the most interesting old buildings standing in Newmarket."

In the hundreds of years after Wentworth Cheswill's death, this storefront has served many purposes. I was asked to record audio for the New Market Historical Society's walking tour, an effort led by John and Kris Carmichael. I was lucky enough to perform the audio script for Cheswill's Store, and, from the script, I learned a lot.

Prior to the mid-1860s, Dr. Benjamin Towle had an office here, but by 1870, Helen Leavitt was in the building teaching music. Ten years later, it was a store again, where John Saunders, an Irish immigrant, sold "boots, shoes and groceries." The audio script explains, "in the space of five years, both John and his wife Bridget, and all three of their sons succumbed to illness and died." The family did have two daughters who survived the illness, Lizzie and Nellie Saunders. They both continued to live in the house next door, renting the old Cheswill storefront for decades more. Matt Kennedy, a close family friend to the Saunders, ran it as a grocery store for 38 years, right up until his death in 1938. By 1940, Kennedy's store had become Marcotte's Market, named for proprieter Ed Marcotte, a French Canadian immigrant. This version of the store lasted right into the 1980s, but neither Matt Kennedy nor Ed Marcotte ever actually owned the building. That we can still enjoy the building is thanks to those Saunders sisters. Nellie, the younger, lived in the adjoining house until the early 1960s, continuously collecting rent from the store started by her father almost a century earlier.

It is a true wonder that a small storefront Wentworth Cheswill established in the 18th century has provided opportunities for commerce right up through the 21st century. In conclusion, please don't graffiti that building again. It's a local treasure.

THE LIBRARIAN

In 1801, Wentworth Cheswill and three other men, Josiah Adams, Nathaniel Rogers, and James Hill, all veterans of the battles of Saratoga, established the Newmarket Social Library through an act approved on June 16, 1801 by the New Hampshire State Senate and House of Representatives in General Court. The library would evolve over many generations, moving from private to public, and their efforts can be traced directly to the creation of the current Newmarket Public Library.

Unlike the library of today, the Newmarket Social Library was a joint stock company for which shareholders paid a modest subscription fee to access its rare commodity: a collection of books. The first free public library in the world would not arrive until 1833. It would be in New Hampshire as well, but, instead of a subscription fee, the Peterborough Town Library was supported by taxation. Wentworth Cheswill's library was supported by membership.

New Market Historical Society president John Carmichael, who is getting a lot of mention in this book, alerted me to a collection of books once held by someone he speculated may have contributed to what became the Newmarket Social Library. Edward Parsons, the first attorney in Newmarket, was a member of General Enoch Poor's regiment in the Continental Army and was killed at Fort Ticonderoga in 1776. His personal estate inventory was attested to on April 20, 1777 by none-other-than Wentworth Cheswill and Josiah Adams, both founders of the Newmarket Social Library. The inventory was taken after the event of Parsons' passing and included "110 volumes and some pamphlets." It is very possible that the two men set aside the late attorney's books and offered them as part of the community's first library.

Wentworth Cheswill was known to maintain a significant personal library himself. After his own passing, he was keen to share his books, with some notable limits. In his last will and testament, in addition to the various legalese for which he was an expert, Wentworth wrote, "I also order and direct that my Library and collection of Manuscripts be kept safe and altogether, by my said wife, for her own use during Life… if any Posterity should desire the Use of any of the Books and give Caution to return the same again in reasonable Time, they may be lent out to them, provided that only one Book be out of said Library in the Hands of any one Heir at the same Time." Frankly it sounds like he didn't trust his children with the books as much as he trusted his wife and paying subscribers. Mary died in 1829, and less than a hundred years later there was only one known book left in the collection.

In 1916, Nellie Palmer George described a book that surely came from Wentworth Cheswill's personal library. The book, which remained in the Cheswill mansion house for almost fifty years after Wentworth's death, was a copy of *The Power of Parliament* published in 1715. Nellie notes that Wentworth Cheswill signed the book himself and a line of cypher rested below his signature. This was probably the characteristic flourish he included when he signed his name, rather than some kind of secret code. It appears that Nellie may have been saving space in her article for the actual title of the book, which was likely: *Of the power of Parliaments. With political observations relating thereunto.*

First issued in 1714 as *Of the antiquity, power & decay of Parliaments*, author Thomas Rymer, who was primarily a literary critic, refocused his sentiments about parliaments for this edition, the third of this book. Rymer died in 1713 so further editions were not undertaken by him personally. Regardless, this is the book Wentworth Cheswill probably had on his shelf. For the final years of his life, Rymer had been a somewhat unpopular royal historian. Thomas Babington Macaulay, who wrote his own five-volume *History of England*, called Rymer "the worst critic that ever lived."

According to Nellie Palmer George, Wentworth Cheswill's copy of the Rymer book included the bookplate of "Edward Mosly." From this detail, it can be inferred that the book traveled across the ocean with Edward Moseley, one of North Carolina's most prominent 18th century politicians. Born and raised in London, Moseley collected a lot of accolades and superlatives during his career as a colonial politician, attorney, and surveyor. He was also a notable collector and curator of books. At his passing, he had over 400 volumes.

Beyond Moseley's bookplate, Wentworth Cheswill's copy also included the signature of Captain Benjamin Torry, who Nellie inferred was the one who gifted the book to Wentworth. There were quite a few men of this name during this time period, but I can't find anyone who rose to the rank of captain. For example, there was Private Benjamin Torry of the New York Militia who fought in the War of 1812. This could be our man, but it could also be any number of Benjamin Torrys in and around New England during this time.

After Cheswill got the book, it sat in his house (available for reading by members of the Newmarket Social Library during his lifetime; available to his heirs after his death) until the mansion house was removed in the 1860s. Nellie's parents were renting the house at the time, and I assume they took the book with them as a memento. Nellie herself appears to have held onto the book through 1916. A lover of history and an admirer of Wentworth Cheswill, Nellie probably had the book in her possession right until her death in 1939. What happened next is a mystery. The book's current whereabouts are unknown.

Up until a few weeks ago, just before this book's publication, that was the end of this chapter. The last known book belonging to Wentworth Cheswill was lost forever, and no other book was known. I pondered that others may be on the bookshelf of a descendent or in circulation in the antiquarian book trade, but that was that.

I am delighted to announce that things have changed.

Nearly two hundred years after the passing of Wentworth Cheswill, another book has been revealed. The owner wishes to remain anonymous but I have held the book in my own hand, and it is undoubtedly genuine. Rest assured that locked away in a family vault rests a copy of 1760's ninth edition of *The Works of the Ingenious Mr. George Farquhar Containing all his Poems, Letters, Essays and Comedies, Publish'd in his Life-time*. The author died in 1707, the year David Lawrence of Exeter drafted a deed promising to one day release Richard (Cheswill) from enslavement.

The book's spine has six compartments with gilt lettered labels. Wentworth Cheswill does not sign the book once, but thrice. In fact, he signs the volume repeatedly in a way that I have never seen him sign his name before. The signatures, two in ink and one in pencil, are undoubtedly authentic, but there is a minor change in how he signs in that he writes *Wentworth Cheswill's*, adding an s to the end of his surname to declare ownership. As for the book's anonymous owner, she presented me with a family tree that clearly reveals her to be a direct descendent of Wentworth Cheswill.

An Irish dramatist, George Farquhar, entered Trinity College at the age of 17 and was kicked out or otherwise left the school, due to what his 18th century biographer called his "gay and volatile disposition." Not cut out for the clergy like his father, he became an actor, but that too was short lived. He was either kicked out or otherwise left the theater after he stabbed a fellow actor with a sword during a production of *The Indian Emperor* by John Dryden, England's first poet laureate. By most accounts, he married a penniless widow, was a poetry addict, and wrote a bunch of bawdy plays full of sexual intrigue and mistaken identities though he is credited as turning away from the more salacious themes with his later plays, giving way to a greater interest in sentimentality.

It seems fitting that Wentworth Cheswill was not only reading about the power and decay of parliamentary government but he was also reading poems and plays. If anything, then we can finally say Wentworth Cheswill had a wide range of reading interests.

THE JUDGE

The New Market Historical Society maintains a collection of Wentworth Cheswill's legal documents from the time he served as Justice of the Peace for New Hampshire's Rockingham County. Many of these documents were purchased in a lot from an antiques dealer in Maine, but the documents were originally recovered from the Exeter town dump many years ago. Writing that last sentence made my blood boil. Other documents have been collected piecemeal.

During the colonial period, the Justice of the Peace was one of the first offices established to maintain order. Incidentally, the town constable was another. The two roles often worked parallel with each other. After the Revolution, the role of Justice of the Peace expanded dramatically. In his post-Revolution role, Wentworth handled civil and criminal cases, often demanding the payment of debts. He even threatened imprisonment if payment was not made in a timely manner. Much of this was done from his mansion house. I have seen a document where Wentworth demands that a man come to his home at exactly ten o'clock in the morning on April 10, 1809 (the day before his birthday) to testify. This calling of defendants to the judge's home was apparently common practice. Imagine judges today demanding people show up at their homes.

Perusing Wentworth Cheswill's legal documents provides a look at the types of people suing each other, from blacksmiths to chairmakers, yeomen to mariners. I saw another document, from 1810, on the online marketplace. It involved a judgment against Colonel Richard Hilton, the direct descendent of one of New Hampshire's first settlers. This is the family that later sold land to Wentworth's grandfather after he was freed from enslavement. Wentworth ruled against him.

Wentworth Cheswill is regarded as the first African American judge, mostly in the descriptions of online auctions that peddle his legal papers. With that said, the superlative may be true. He was elected in 1805.

When I first started my research, these legal documents would appear in these auctions, selling for under $100. I acquired a signed judgment from Wentworth Cheswill for $50 and displayed the document in a glass case in the Newmarket Mills. At the time of this writing, it is still there for the public to view. Nowadays, these documents often appear with buy-it-now prices ranging from $1000 to $3000. I regret that my efforts to spread the word about the Cheswills may have contributed to this inflation. Surely this book you are holding right now will not help the matter. I speculate that a legal document recently offered by Sotheby's may have been paraphrasing several articles and biographical summaries I have released over the years. Regardless, every year another example of Wentworth Cheswill's signature pops up and the asking price only gets higher and higher.

I hope some of these artifacts make it back to Newmarket and the New Market Historical Society. If you ever want to see one for free, then I encourage you to visit the Stone School Museum. We have a bunch of them. Take a look at America's Crow Bar while you are there.

THE CHILDREN

As a school teacher, I can assure you that one can learn quite a lot about people through the interests and temperament of their children. While it isn't always the case that our kids are composites of ourselves (and certainly they shouldn't be), many don't fall far from the tree.

The Cheswills, Wentworth and Mary, had eleven children thrive beyond infancy, though thirteen were born in all. Details are scarce on some of them, but others are well documented. Surely some can tell us about the nature of their parents. At least one was a religious and community leader. Others were farmers. Some were married and have descendents living today. Others remained unmarried.

Again, the Cheswills had thirteen children in all with two not surviving infancy. Their first child Paul was born on August 4, 1768, eleven months after their wedding and the very year Wentworth was made town constable. Paul grew up to live on sixty acres of farmland given to him by his father off Dame Road. He died January 19, 1832. At the time of this writing, Paul's graveyard is sadly in extreme disrepair. It rests behind the Wade Farm Condos.

Thomas was born next on July 20, 1770. He attended Phillips Exeter Academy and later became a deacon. He would grow up to live in Hopestill's house at Moonlight Bridge. Recently I saw a book up for auction that had the signature of Thomas in it. In fact, he signed the title page repeatedly just as his father had done with the book of Irish plays. The book was volume two of *The Works of Mr. John Glas*, who started a religious movement in Scotland that argued for abandoning Presbyterian principles of Church government and adopting Congregationalist views instead. This particular volume was printed during John Glas's lifetime in 1761. At the time, I was hoping that Thomas might have inherited the book from his father so I could finally hold a tome from the library of Wentworth Cheswill himself. Alas, there was no signature from him, but ironically it was also signed by Eliphalet Merrill, who compiled the *Gazetteer of New Hampshire* that I quote early in this book with regards to the Aurora-borealis.

While it is hard to determine whether the content is from Eliphalet or Thomas's hand, there is also a page of handwriting in the book that speculates on the musings of John Milton, author of *Paradise Lost*. The author of the note, written in the book's liner pages, discussed the second coming, the upcoming millennium, and even the end of the world. At one point, the writer mentions that, according to Milton, the end of everything would begin "in the year of our Lord 1842" with Jesus Christ physically appearing and casting judgment upon the world. Thomas died in 1841.

The Cheswills' next four children were Samuel (1772), Sarah (1774), Mary (1775), and Elizabeth (1778). All lived well into adulthood except for Elizabeth who died at the age of 21. Sarah would marry and have a son that would become a prominent businessman and president of the Cheswell Cotton mill of South Carolina.

Nancy (1780) and Mehitable (1782) followed their siblings. Mehitable's daughter would marry into the Mathes family, who were among the very first European settlers in New Hampshire. Her husband Benjamin Mathes Jr will come up again shortly.

The Cheswills buried an unnamed daughter in 1785. Their son William was born the same year.

Next to be born was Martha (1788), another daughter who did not survive (1792), and then finally Abigail, also born in 1792.

Martha Cheswell (the spelling changes with her generation) was the last family member to be in possession of the immediate family's estate. She is the one who rented out the mansion house to Nellie Palmer George's parents. It is Martha's name that graces the gate at the Cheswill Family Graveyard. The gate was placed in 1861. When she passed away in 1867, in her will, Martha deeded the mansion house to her two nephews John Perkins and John W. Smart. Curiously there seems to have been some contention about her father Wentworth Cheswill's journal. It does not appear that Martha ever married or had children of her own, but she left her books and papers to Benjamin Mathes Jr, the husband of one of her nieces. A case was brought to court shortly after her death concerning some bank notes. In it, there is also reference to the plaintiffs, John Perkins and another, presumably John W. Smart, inquiring "whether she said anything, and if so what, about a journal kept by her father, which she thought the family would like to preserve." What came of the journal from the court case is unclear, but Wentworth Cheswill's commonplace book would eventually make its way to the University of New Hampshire's archives by way of the papers of Roland Douglas Sawyer, a Congregationalist minister and Massachusetts state legislator. Sawyer spent his last years living in the nearby town of Kensington working on local history research projects. How he came upon it is a mystery.

Eventually John Perkins sold his portion of the family land to the other nephew, John W. Smart. It would be John W. Smart, Wentworth Cheswill's grandson, who would decide to remove the Cheswill mansion house in the 1860s. When exactly this happened (or even why) is unclear, but the home he built in its place still exists today. The odd thing is that the house is on Packers Falls Road where it was moved in 1912 by then-owner Edwin Carpenter.

As the story goes, a 1912 barn fire damaged the John W. Smart home, so Edwin decided to move the house to Packers Falls Road. He built yet another new home in the original spot. The third and final structure built on the same site was completed in 1913. It was constructed for Edwin's new wife Laurel Bell Hendrix, after his first wife Harriet Mudge passed away. This final home on the old Cheswill mansion house foundation still exists today. It is the house where Richard Alperin lived when he first learned of Wentworth Cheswill and became inspired to restore the family cemetery and get the historical marker placed. It would be that historical marker that would one day inspire me.

Descendents of the Cheswills continued to shape the town for many years, even indirectly. For example, Millie, the wife of Wentworth's great-great grandson, William Thomas Cheswell, sued to acquire land willed to her late husband's father, William Oliver Cheswell. When Oliver came of age he inherited the house, taking ownership from his mother, who got her husband's plaid coat in exchange. Millie won the lawsuit and a year later sold the property to the Newmarket School District. It became the site of what is now Newmarket Jr/Sr High School, where my son and (soon) my daughter are enrolled.

Edwin Carpenter's family continued to own all of the Cheswill land across the street from the school. Edwin's grandson John operated Carpenter's Olde English Florist there. My family regularly visited its weekly farmers' market. Eventually the land was sold and made into a school parking lot.

THE PORTRAIT

There are no known contemporary portraits of Wentworth Cheswill. Now that I have held a book from his famed library, it is a portrait that has become the artifact I most hope will someday come to light. One may still be in an antique shop or a Cheswill descendent's attic, its significance unknown.

A lack of portraiture has caused Wentworth to suffer the same fate of a number of celebrated historical figures in that we simply don't know what he looked like. For example, there are no known portraits of William Shakespeare. Of course many portraits and statues of Shakespeare exist, but they all seem to be inspired by a small, reworked posthumous portrait. Wentworth Cheswill has not enjoyed the same creative license from his admirers. Instead people have inexplicably used the portraits of others to represent him.

Sacagawea, guide of the Lewis and Clark Expedition, has been memorialized many times—even though there are no known contemporary portraits of her either. It isn't just her face that is a mystery. Historians can't agree on the dates of her birth or death. Even her real name is up for debate. Despite all this, Sacagawea was minted on an American dollar coin and is the subject of over a dozen statues. Her face is prominently shown with all these memorials, depicted with mindful respect to her family and culture. Wentworth Cheswill has not enjoyed the same recognition.

Individuals in the New Hampshire State Legislature argued that a lack of contemporary portraiture is the very reason why they would not vote to create a painting of Wentworth Cheswill to hang in the State House. As of this writing, of the two hundred and thirteen portraits in the New Hampshire State House, there is not a single portrait of a person of color—and it is not for a lack of trying. One was proposed for Wentworth Cheswill, but lawmakers successfully argued against it as recently as 2022.

A quick web search produces several images claiming to be Wentworth Cheswill, but the portraits are almost always of other people. For example, there is a portrait of Barzillai Lew, another revolutionary soldier of African descent. The actual painting hangs in the diplomatic reception room of the State Department, but, for some reason, this image comes up regularly with the claim that it is Wentworth Cheswill. The subject holds a flute in the portrait which is not even blurred out when it is presented as him. Barzillai and his wife Dinah were both talented musicians. To my knowledge, while Wentworth Cheswill was prolific and inspiring in many ways, playing the flute was not one of them.

Another person's face often misrepresented as the face of Wentworth Cheswill is that of revolutionary double agent James Armistead Lafayette. Born into enslavement, he lived much of his life on a Virginia plantation, but, during the revolution, he enlisted in the

Marquis de Lafayette's French allied unit as a spy. He even worked with the notorious turncoat, Benedict Arnold.

Other individuals presented as Wentworth Cheswill have included abolitionist and social reformer Fredrick Douglas as well as William Harvey Carney, one of the twenty-two African Americans to receive the Medal of Honor for his service during the Civil War.

So, what did Wentworth Cheswill actually look like?

It does not escape me that race is a social construct, but references to his race are all we have to go on. In 1767, the census recorded the landowning, well positioned school teacher as white—despite his father being a prominent person of color recorded as "mulatto." It has been suggested to me more than once that the community had no other choice but to list the prominent mixed race man as white to avoid any uncomfortable perceptions. Three years after Wentworth Cheswill's death he was called "yellow" on the floor of the United States Congress, and he was later included in William Cooper Nell's 1855 *Colored Patriots of the Revolution.*

Perspectives on Wentworth Cheswill's race have fluctuated from generation to generation, reminding me how different people have regarded the Dumas family throughout history. Alexandre Dumas, the author of *The Three Musketeers*, also had a mixed race background. He was considered black when he was alive, white after he died, and black again by most of today's critics. His father Thomas Alexandre Dumas, like Hopestill Cheswill, was considered half black, half white, though he was described in his earliest known description, an 1797 account quoted by historian Tom Reiss in *The Black Count*, as "'something closer to ebony' than to 'bronze.'" Just like Hopestill, Thomas had an enslaved African parent.

Much closer to home, the Cheswill family had a similar racial background to the family of Ona Judge, a person I mentioned earlier. Ona's mother Betty was a bi-racial woman enslaved by the Washingtons. Ona liberated herself and was forced to live as a fugitive while only a couple towns over, Wentworth Cheswill, was living freely as one of the most prosperous and influential men in his community.

Ultimately I am determined to fill in just enough space so that the man himself, Wentworth Cheswill, can come into focus, even if I do not know what he looked like. Hopefully by the end of this slim volume you are more acquainted with him and his family, but, without a contemporary portrait, I cannot describe his appearance with any confidence. Despite that, I strongly believe in creatively imagining those we as a community wish to honor and remember.

The many people who question the very creation of images of Wentworth Cheswill do not seem moved to criticize others whose faces have been creatively interpreted throughout history. I mentioned Sacagawea, who has no known portrait from her lifetime yet is remembered with many portraits and statues. The image of Sacagawea with her infant son, Jean Baptiste Charbonneau, which graced American dollar coins starting in 2000, was designed by sculptor Glenna Goodacre and modeled on Randy'L He-dow Teton, despite having no relation to the original subject.

Christopher Columbus is another historical figure who has no known authentic likeness. There are many portraits and statues of him too. Henry Hudson, the celebrated explorer and navigator, has numerous statues depicting him as well, despite there being no known available likenesses of him from his lifetime. Lakota leader Crazy Horse, who has no portrait from his lifetime, has inspired a massive mountain-side image which has been under construction since 1948. When completed, it will depict the man riding a horse and pointing to his tribal land. It is an impressively grand memorial commissioned to be sculpted by Korczak Ziolkowski.

In honor of Wenworth Cheswill's 275th birthday, I too created art to counter all the misrepresentations I found on the Internet. I carved a block print of him atop his horse. For years, I have offered these prints to those who have made considerable contributions to the cause of spreading the word about him. I also illustrated a comic strip that I freely distribute to anyone who wants a copy, including my fifth grade daughter's classmates. I encourage artists to continue to make images that honor those they wish to remember, including Wentworth Cheswill.

THE VOLCANO

On the 5th of April, 1815, Mount Tambora in the Dutch East Indies, now Indonesia, erupted. Nearly ten cubic miles of pyroclastic trachyandesite entered the stratosphere during the largest volcanic eruption recorded in human history. Whatever Wentworth Cheswill was doing that day, he was surely unaware of the eruption that would parallel the end of his life.

On that day, a sulfate aerosol veil, a sun-blocking cloud, turned the sky from day to night as earthquakes triggered tsunamis. Tens of thousands of people died in the days that followed. Famine, caused by the disrupted sunlight's effect on crop yields, killed many more around the globe in the coming years.

In a villa in the Swiss Alps, the dismal weather created by volcanic haze inspired Mary Shelly, age eighteen, to write what would become *Frankenstein; or, The Modern Prometheus.* In it, she wrote, "It was already one in the morning; the rain pattered dismally against the panes, and my candle was nearly out, when, by the glimmer of the half-extinguished light, I saw the dull yellow eye of the creature open."

In South West England, artist John Constable painted the oppressive weather caused by the volcanic haze as it appeared during his honeymoon. In his painting, anxiety inducing clouds churn above small figures on the beach along Weymouth Bay.

On May 17, 1816, Thomas Jefferson, from his home at Monticello, wrote with the suspicious tone of one on the edge of a great discovery: "The spring has been unusually dry and cold. Our average morning cold for the month of May in other years has been 63° of Farenheit. In the present month it has been to this day an average of 53° and one morning as low as 43°. Repeated frosts have killed the early fruits and the crops of tobacco and wheat will be poor." Jefferson never drew the conclusion that it was a volcano that had dramatically altered the Earth's climate. A haze, like a mourning veil, was traveling across the world.

In Germany, the cost of feeding and maintaining a horse during these trying times became so difficult, Karl Drais invented an alternative means of transportation. His Laufmaschine became what we know as the bicycle.

In New England, a half a foot of snow fell in June of 1816. The year was nicknamed "the poverty year" or "eighteen hundred and froze-to-death." It is now often remembered as *The Year Without a Summer.* This would be the final year of Wentworth Cheswill's life.

In his seventies, Wentworth Cheswill was signing legal writs mere weeks before his death. At this time, he had jurisdiction over petty civil matters. His legal papers, which I mentioned still exist in the dozens, don't tell us much about the man, but they do tell us about the time he lived in. In case after case, he offered judgment. With his meticulous handwriting, he threatened jail or otherwise demanded people come to his "dwelling" to give their side of each altercation or mishap. He dealt with continuous complaints about a lack of payment for services. These conflicts kept him engaged right up until the moment he became gravely ill.

Between the fall of 1815 and his death in early 1817, Wentworth Cheswill did not experience the joy of a warm summer day. The volcano took that away. The stately elms that populated his estate saw their leaves drop early due to the extreme weather. His crops surely yielded less food compared to previous seasons. Those around him, who were almost universally less fortunate, would have struggled, but he probably remained comfortable in his mansion house, warm but worried. As those around New England became despondent, desperate, and hungry, what did he think? What did he do? His community regarded him as wise and they looked to him for guidance. Right to his end, they probably looked to him for hope. During this time, his son Thomas was the elected selectman and "overseer of the poor." At the time of his death, Wentworth Cheswill was one of the wealthiest men in town.

On March 8, 1817, Seth Shackford, a neighbor of the Cheswill family, wrote in his journal, "Esquire Wentworth Cheswell died about two o'clock today of typhus fever."

Based on the incubation of typhus, Wentworth Cheswill would have contracted the illness two weeks earlier from the bite of a flea, mite, louse, or tick. There is a legal document in the possession of the New Market Historical Society, one of Wentworth's many judgments as Justice of the Peace, which reveals he was still working just weeks before his death. He would have experienced a fever, headache, and probably a rash. At the age of seventy-one, and without the benefits of modern medicine, the illness would be too much for him.

A year earlier, the community of Cape Cod experienced a bout of typhus that killed seventy-two members of Eastham alone. We don't know what treatment Wentworth Cheswill accepted, but, whatever it was, it was unlikely anything that comforted him. Doctors of his era were often poisoning their patients with mercury or conducting counterproductive procedures, such as bloodletting. None of this would have helped against typhus.

No amount of money or influence would have helped Wentworth Cheswill. In 1799, after contracting a sore throat, doctors drew George Washington's blood four times. Before he died, they gave him an enema and induced vomiting. After two days of so-called medical treatment, Washington was dead, surrounded by his wife, several trusted friends, three enslaved housemaids, and an enslaved valet. How Wentworth Cheswill was treated in his final days is a mystery, but his wife Mary and several of his children were no doubt present.

The moment of Wentworth Cheswill's death was recorded in his neighbor's personal diary mere hours after his last breath. We can infer that his demise was news well beyond Newmarket. Dr. John Farmer, the father of systematic genealogy in America and the editor of Jeremy Belknap's first volume of the *History of New Hampshire*, would note that "Wentworth Cheswell, Esquire (a colored man) died in Newmarket in 1817, aged seventy-one. He was a man of considerable information and furnished Dr. Belknap with information for his history of New Hampshire."

So began a long history of remembrance.

On April 29, following Wentworth Cheswill's death, Mary, his widow, posted a notice in the *New Hampshire Gazette* encouraging the customary act of those indebted to the estate to make their case known, and those with debts to the estate to pay them. Such a public notice was common practice. One would expect that after such a notice mentions of him would gradually diminish over time. His loved ones, friends and family, would remember him fondly, but the rest of the world would move on in the years and decades to come.

Except this was not the case.

In 1820, three years after his death, Wentworth Cheswill was name dropped in an argument by Senator David Morril against discriminatory racial legislation before the United States Congress. He reminisced that, "In New Hampshire, there was a yellow man by the name of Cheswell, who, with his family, was respectable in point of abilities, property, and character. He held some of the first offices of the town..." Morril, from Epping, New Hampshire, a town southwest of Newmarket, invoked Wentworth's name during the congressional debate over the Missouri Compromise. Politician William Plummer would use the memory of Wentworth in a similar argument. Both men would argue that Wentworth Cheswill represented a strong reason why racial discrimination was simply preposterous. Both men, Morril and Plummer, would become governors of New Hampshire.

Twenty five years later, Wentworth Cheswill was mentioned in William Cooper Nell's *Colored Patriots of the Revolution*, which paraphrased Morril's speech, noting that (Wentworth Cheswill) "a colored man" had "held some of the first offices of the town in which he resided, was appointed Justice of the Peace for the county, and was perfectly competent to perform all the duties of his various offices in the most prompt, accurate, and acceptable manner." David Morril had taken the argument a step further, making the point that: "...this family are forbidden to enter and live in Missouri."

Close to a hundred years later, Wentworth Cheswill was still being mentioned. In articles from 1906, 1908, and 1916, his accolades were still being listed, detailed, and embellished. It was during this time period that he was likened to "the immortal Revere." The comparison to Paul Revere appeared close to a hundred years after he passed away, and he is still often referred to as the "Black Paul Revere"—even today.

In the first decade of the 20th century, Newmarket historian Nellie Palmer George published her six page remembrance of Wentworth Cheswill's mansion house, which had been demolished a half century earlier. There aren't many people, living or dead, who merit a multi-page posthumous remembrance of their house, but Wentworth Cheswill was deemed worthy of this recognition. The article also included a biography and featured a list of the many of the public offices he served in, how he "held the esteem and confidence of his fellow townsmen," and how he "died lamented."

The Newmarket Club of Boston, a social club of the early 20th century said of Wentworth Cheswill (a hundred years after his death) that, "The records left to us of those years are meager but they tell plainly of the esteem and confidence with which his fellow citizens looked up to the man whose wise counsel, clear outlook and untiring energy was ever at their service." What an honor to be remembered so long after one's death for simply being a good person. To them, Wentworth was Newmarket's Town Father, an example of public service and community commitment to aspire to.

In 1939, Cheswill descendents were proudly self-identified in an article about the placement of a stone marker at the site of the Smith-Davis Garrison, once home to the English ancestors of Wentworth's wife, Mary Davis.

On November 23, 1945, the Portsmouth Herald reported that, "Citizens of Newmarket have been aroused by the mysterious disappearance of the beautifully designed wrought iron gate from the Cheswell cemetery on Main Street. The oldest cemetery in Newmarket, it was known for many years as the burying ground of the descendents of Wentworth Cheswell, businessman and town father in the late 1700s. Police and caretakers are searching for the gate which has the family name inscribed in its center." The gate would return (and remains in place today), even while the family, inducing Newmarket's Town Father, buried therein, was about to be forgotten.

Allow me to amend that last statement. Wentworth Cheswill was never entirely forgotten.

While there was a long period of relative silence, his archaeological efforts were profiled in a 1980 issue of *The New Hampshire Archeologist*, a publication of the New Hampshire Archeological Society. The piece, written by historians Dennis Chesley and Mary Beth McAllister, revealed Wentworth's fascination with history. The article quoted his personal letters to Jeremy Belknap which recounted his investigations into the remains of indigenous populations as far as Ossipee, fifty miles away.

A decade after that, Erik Tuveson wrote his paper *A People of Color: A Study of Race and Racial Identification in New Hampshire 1750-1825* which included an in depth and informative focus on the Cheswill family. Surely thanks to Tuveson, more academic mentions would follow. There would also be an increase in Wentworth Cheswill mentions in local history books, though public awareness remained relatively slim.

Wentworth Cheswill's folk hero status dimmed dramatically in the early to mid 20th century. His long held reverence faded fast. For all intents and purposes, he became a curious historical footnote, even to those who lived beside his cemetery.

What is clear is that for at least a hundred years after his death Wentworth Cheswill had been fairly well known. Tales about him and his family were passed down for generations. Often compared to Paul Revere, Wentworth Cheswill was a local folk hero—until something changed. Public awareness diminished, and, by the turn of the millennium, for the first time in several hundred years, he was relatively unknown. His family cemetery was abandoned to the natural elements. Thirteen trees grew within its stone wall boundary. Its grave stones were cracked and toppled. Some were hidden beneath the ground, lost to neglect and the passage of time—just like the men and women buried beneath them.

But a spark was ignited by a letter.

The wife of a Cheswill descendant from Sacramento, California sent a letter to Newmarket resident Richard Alperin, who, at the time, unknowingly lived on the site of the old Cheswill mansion house. The letter inquired about the upkeep of the family cemetery, which had fallen into disrepair decades earlier. Alerted and inspired, Alperin, over several years, and alongside more Cheswill descendants, local historians, and the New Hampshire Old Graveyard Association, went on to restore the cemetery, going so far as to replicate and replace Wentworth Cheswill's damaged gravestone. Richard Alperin is also responsible for the roadside historical marker installed in October of 2007, which, in turn, sparked my own interest when I drove by.

The morning after I presented the initial culmination of my research, my poem, *Wentworth Cheswill's Ride*, a title I repurposed for this book, I was invited to join the board of the New Market Historical Society. Soon after that, I asked the other directors what happened to erase such an interesting person from public memory, especially in the town he so loved. How could a community forget their Town Father? One director speculated to me that mid-century cultural conflict concerning race may have been a strong factor in erasing the once celebrated Cheswills from public awareness.

Could a loss of history happen that quickly?

Perhaps I have overlooked something, but I cannot find a mention of Wentworth Cheswill in the 1950s. For ten years there were little to no publications or recognitions of the Cheswill family publicly recorded. A Cheswill descendent later said to me that some of her own ancestors may have contributed to the silence. For a while, she speculated that it may have been taboo to talk about her family's history of enslavement. For whatever reason, Wentworth's folk hero status faded quickly just when it should have been rising.

It wouldn't be until 1966 that locals founded the New Market Historical Society. "Doc" Dr. L. (Leonard) Forbes Getchell and Sylvia Getchell, husband and wife, lead a vibrant return to historical appreciation in the community. As current society president John Carmichael writes in a dedication found on the society's webpage, "Their mission spotlighted the rich historic fabric of this small village, and they instilled a pride in the community which had been lost for decades. 'Doc' and Sylvia Getchell were founding members of the New Market Historical Society in 1966; their leadership, knowledge and energy helped create a dynamic organization which culminated in the Town's celebrated 250th Anniversary in 1977."

One of the society's earliest missions was to collect items with Newmarket-specific historical significance. People searched their attics, basements, and barns and filled the two floors of the 1843 Stone School, which had been acquired by the society for a dollar for the purpose of a headquarters and museum. This organization and its efforts to preserve the history of the community would set the stage for a Wentworth Cheswill comeback in the years to come, but the local history publications that came out of this era, including those written by Sylvia Getchell, herself a local treasure, barely mentioned the Cheswills at all.

It is important to note here that the existence of Wentworth Cheswill's journal was probably not known to the Getchells or others during the earliest years of the historical society. Roland Douglas Sawyer, the minister whose personal papers, collected in a hundred and sixty-five archival boxes, the journal included in one of them, gave those papers to the University of New Hampshire after his death. He died at the age of ninety-five in 1969. By the way, this guy, Roland Douglas Sawyer, was a real collector. Thirteen more boxes—mostly containing his collection of dime novels—are at the Athenaeum of Philadelphia.

In the run up to Wentworth Cheswill's 275th birthday I went public with a project I called the Wentworth Cheswill Appreciation Society. It started as a grandiose title for my otherwise humble efforts to educate the public. Years later, this book is a continuation of that work. Most of my plans were dashed as the first year of my project is more commonly remembered as the first year of the COVID-19 global pandemic, but I did accomplish a few remote press and event appearances. I spoke to audiences about Wentworth Cheswill, albeit remotely, through online video streams. I made art, including a comic strip and a commemorative block print. I stood outdoors in the Cheswill cemetery, briefly removing my mask to be interviewed for public radio. A group of us were even charged with exploring the establishment of a public monument for Wentworth Cheswill. Early meetings were held outside at picnic tables. It seemed like things were finally happening, even as the world was in isolation.

After the public radio appearance, I was messaged anonymously and strongly admonished. Without mincing words, I was told that only Black people should learn or care about Wentworth Cheswill. I was also told that I was doing damage to the community in my efforts to replace and rewrite history. I was mortified. I discreetly sought advice from an old friend, Tito Jackson, former president of the Black Student Union at the University of New Hampshire. Back in November of 1998, Tito helped lead around sixty Black students in a takeover of the University president's office for a silent protest. It was the final act in a long history of what the BSU had deemed "Broken Promises," which was the title of the document listing their twelve demands, including curriculum reform and the increased hiring of Black faculty. After I explained my project on Wentworth Cheswill, without hesitation, Tito encouraged me to keep going. He reminded me how especially important it was for everyone, regardless of race, to feel empowered to honor and remember people of color.

Incidentally, back in 1998, among those protesting Black students, there was a white male student. He had helped edit that "Broken Promises" document, working all the previous night in a small room in the school's Memorial Union Building. He was an English major, and he felt like it was the best way he could help. When the actual sit-in approached, he was told he didn't have to get involved—as there may be arrests. He showed up anyway. He of course was me. My father called me the next day and told me he saw me on TV. He was startled. He didn't know what to say other than, "Try not to get arrested, but give them hell." I guess it makes sense that the book I am publishing now as an adult is about the first person of African descent elected to public office. I learned at University of New Hampshire that it is critically important that white people feel comfortable sharing Black stories.

THE FOLK HERO

By what criteria does a community decide who gets a statue, a painting, a street, or a plaza? Folk heroes represent our highest ideals.

To be worthy of remembrance, one must possess qualities that capture the imagination. They become a symbol of hope, a reminder that one person can make a difference. Folk heroes are often ordinary people who exhibited extraordinary courage or resilience at their own peril.

The facts surrounding their lives are also often a bit fuzzy.

Johnny "Appleseed" Chapman, who planted trees in Illinois, has been regarded for generations as a champion of conservation. The real life John Chapman was a follower of Swedenborgianism, the teachings of mystic Emanuel Swedenborg, an individual who Victor Hugo referenced in Chapter 14 of *Les Miserables* as having "glided into insanity." No offense to Swedenborgianists but I mention it as this interesting personal detail was not mentioned in the poem that helped make Johnny Appleseed famous, 1881's *Apple-Seed John* by Lydia Maria Child.

Another notable folk hero, John Henry, famously competed with a steam engine to cut a railroad tunnel into the side of a mountain in Virginia (or maybe Alabama). The location of the event that made him famous is not agreed upon, but that does not stop the continued remembrance of him. We know only from his folk tale that he beat the engine, dying shortly thereafter. To this day, he embodies the rivalry between humankind and industrialization, a dichotomy that has become timeless. He is featured in numerous children's books.

Folk heroes are often charismatic figures. In New Hampshire, we have a folk hero named Passaconaway, who convinced early European colonists that he possessed mysterious powers. Legend has it that he swam across the Merrimack River under water in a single breath. At the Amoskeag Falls in Manchester, people witnessed him make trees dance. He could make water burn and move rocks without any apparent force of hand. There is a historically inaccurate commemorative statue of him in Lowell, Massachusetts. It presents him in a headdress traditionally worn by the indigenous people of the American Plains.

With feats legendary but facts dim, all three, Johnny Appleseed, John Henry, and Passaconway, are folk heroes. They are celebrated by their deeds as much as what they represent to their communities. And all three are remembered creatively with illustrations, poetry, and statues.

Folk heroes are surrounded by mythology because they embody who we want to aspire to. We embellish them so that they can reflect our ideals. They become vessels for community values and the lessons we wish to teach our young. I think of the heroism and self sacrifice of folk hero Molly Pitcher, who carried water to soldiers during the Revolutionary War's Battle of Monmouth. According to legend, she replaced her husband in battle when he couldn't fight anymore. The issue is that Molly Pitcher is based on Mary Ludwig Hays McCarthy. At the time, Molly was a nickname for Mary. "Pitcher" came from the water she carried. The problem is that she does not appear to have been around during that battle. The story emerged after her death.

As I spend these pages debunking rumors and misconceptions about Wentworth Cheswill—of which there was a great deal—my fear is that I have provided the argument against remembering him. For in the end, he was just a man. To demystify him serves to take away his legendary status. Or does it? Maintaining folk heroism seems to hinge on one's lasting positive impact, as well as what one individual can inspire in others. Debunking the legends only seems to strengthen his story. Perhaps Wentworth Cheswill could become a new type of folk hero. The ideals he represents are certainly ideals that we should aspire to in the 21st century.

Wentworth Cheswill embodies the virtues of community service, leadership, and an unwavering commitment to the well-being of our fellow citizens. Though he is one of the earliest of African descent elected to public office in the United States, his legacy goes well beyond that. He had a lifelong dedication to the betterment of his community. Serving as a town messenger, constable, assessor, selectman, teacher, judge, soldier, just to name a few, he went beyond the mere fulfillment of those duties. His life work was making his community better. For generations, he was a symbol for breaking barriers and creating a better world for future generations. His passions were the foundations for a better tomorrow, including a special reverence for history, education, literacy, community, and liberty. This is his legacy.

Through Wentworth Cheswill and his fascinating family, we have the ability to learn new, enriching perspectives about the origins of America. Whatever stalled his path to folk hero status should not have the final say. In a way, we need Wentworth Cheswill now more than ever. Whether he ever has a portrait hanging in the New Hampshire State House or a statue in the town he helped shape, I choose to remember him by his name. To me, he was more than just the "Black Paul Revere." To me, he is more than just a curious footnote in history. To me, he is an inspiring person who just passed through, riding off just as I arrived to greet him. In a way, we all just missed him.

Of the many accolades and superlatives he gathered over the centuries, I have always been fond of the simple title bestowed upon Wentworth Cheswill by the late Deacon Joseph Judkins in his 1770 last will and testament. In it, Judkins refers to his wife, children, and other associates by name, but when he refers to Wentworth Cheswill, and only him, does he use the term "my friend."

Here's to you, my friend.

ABOUT THE AUTHOR

John Herman is an artist, writer, and teacher. He has the unique experience of being first in an online search for "nerd of all media." He lives with his family in Newmarket, New Hampshire. Learn more at johnherman.org

FURTHER READINGS

Miscellaneous revolutionary documents of New Hampshire : including the association test, the pension rolls, and other important papers by Albert Stillman Batchellor

Jefferson and Science by Silvio Bedini

Cow Hampshire, New Hampshire's History Blog by Janice Brown

Pioneers in New Hampshire Archaeology: Wentworth Cheswill, Esquire by W. Dennis Chesley and Mary Beth McAllister, *New Hampshire Archeologist*

The First Century of Dummer Academy; A Historical Discourse, Delivered at Newbury, Byfield Parish, August 12, 1863 by Nehemiah Cleaveland

Wentworth, Benning (1696–1770) by David E. Van Deventer, *Oxford Dictionary of National Biography*

The Works of the Ingenious Mr. George Farquhar Containing all his Poems, Letters, Essays and Comedies, Publish'd in his Life-time, 1760 edition

Slavery in New Hampshire: Profitable godliness to racial consciousness by Jody R. Fernald

On the Road North of Boston: New Hampshire Taverns and Turnpikes, 1700-1900 by Donna-Belle Garvin and James L. Garvin

Old Newmarket, New Hampshire; historical sketches by Nellie Palmer George

Davis-Smith Garrison by B.B.P. Greene

The Minister's Black Veil by Nathaniel Hawthorne

Encyclopedia of African American History, 1619-1895 by Graham Russell Hodges, edited by Paul Finkleman

Quarterly Bulletin of the Archeological Society of Virginia by C. G. Holland

The Legend of Sleepy Hollow by Washington Irving

The Black Presence in the Era of the American Revolution by Sidney Kaplan

Jefferson, War and Peace, 1776 to 1784 by Marie Kimball

African American Historic Burial Grounds and Gravesites of New England by Glen Knoblock

Paul Revere's Ride by Henry Wadsworth Longfellow

The 'Obama before Obama' by Kevin Merida, *Washington Post*

Gazetteer of the State of New Hampshire by Eliphalet Merrill

Salmagundi by James Kirke Paulding, Vol 3 Issue 12

Military History of New Hampshire 1623 to 1861 by Chandler Eastman Potter

The Black Count by Tom Reiss

Historically Speaking: The life and times of Oxford Tash by Barbara Rimkunas, *Seacoast Online*

Any and all works by J. Dennis Robinson

Of the power of Parliaments. With political observations relating thereunto by Thomas Rymer

Black Portsmouth: Three Centuries of African-American Heritage by Mark J. Sammons and Valerie Cunningham

The Real "Obama before Obama" by Daniel Sauerwein, *History News Network*

The Archeology of New Hampshire by David R. Starbuck

A People of Color: A Study of Race and Racial Identification in New Hampshire 1750-1825 by Erik Tuveson

Biographical Sketches of the Moody Family, Embracing Notices of Ten Ministers and Several Laymen from 1633 to 1842

Proceedings of the M. W. Grand Lodge of the Ancient and Honorable Fraternity of Free and Accepted Masons

Sketch of New Market, Town Directory 1872

History of Newmarket by the Newmarket Club of Boston, published serially in the *Newmarket Advertiser*

Historic American Buildings Survey: Moody Parsonage from the Library of Congress

McClary Place, from the *Manchester Union*

www.ingramcontent.com/pod-product-compliance
Lightning Source LLC
Chambersburg PA
CBHW030847090426
42737CB00009B/1128